WARRIOR • 145

OTTOMAN INFANTRYMAN 1914–18

DAVID NICOLLE

ILLUSTRATED BY CHRISTA HOOK

Series editors Marcus Cowper and Nikolai Bogdanovic

First published in Great Britain in 2010 by Osprey Publishing
Midland House, West Way, Botley, Oxford OX2 0PH, UK
44-02 23rd St, Suite 219, Long Island City, NY 11101, USA
E-mail: info@ospreypublishing.com

A CIP catalog record for this book is available from the British Library

ISBN: 978 184603 506 7

E-book ISBN: 978 1 84908 261 7

Editorial by Ilios Publishing Ltd, Oxford, UK (www.iliospublishing.com)
Cartography: Map Studio, Romsey
Page layout by: Mark Holt
Index by: Alison Worthington
Typeset in Sabon and Myriad Pro
Originated by PPS Grasmere Ltd
Printed in China through Worldprint Ltd

10 11 12 13 14 10 9 8 7 6 5 4 3 2 1

ARTIST'S NOTE

Readers may care to note that the original paintings from which the
colour plates in this book were prepared are available for private sale.
The Publishers retain all reproduction copyright whatsoever.
All enquiries should be addressed to:

Scorpio Gallery,
PO Box 475,
Hailsham,
East Sussex BN27 2SL,
UK

The Publishers regret that they can enter into no correspondence upon
this matter.

THE WOODLAND TRUST

Osprey Publishing are supporting the Woodland Trust, the UK's leading
woodland conservation charity, by funding the dedication of trees.

FOR A CATALOGUE OF ALL BOOKS PUBLISHED BY OSPREY
MILITARY AND AVIATION PLEASE CONTACT:

Osprey Direct, c/o Random House Distribution Center,
400 Hahn Road, Westminster, MD 21157
Email: uscustomerservice@ospreypublishing.com

Osprey Direct, The Book Service Ltd, Distribution Centre,
Colchester Road, Frating Green, Colchester, Essex, CO7 7DW
E-mail: customerservice@ospreypublishing.com

www.ospreypublishing.com

CONTENTS

INTRODUCTION 4

CHRONOLOGY 5

ENLISTMENT 11

TRAINING 16

DAILY LIFE 22

APPEARANCE AND WEAPONRY 28

BELIEF AND BELONGING 34

LIFE ON CAMPAIGN 38

THE SOLDIER IN BATTLE 49

MUSEUMS, RE-ENACTMENT AND COLLECTING 58

BIBLIOGRAPHY 60

GLOSSARY 61

INDEX 64

OTTOMAN INFANTRYMAN 1914–1918

INTRODUCTION

The Ottoman Empire's involvement in World War I, when it allied itself with Germany and the other Central Powers against its traditional ally, Britain, can be traced back beyond the 'Young Turk' revolution of 1908. However, that event brought to power a group of enthusiastic patriots, mainly military officers, who, when they failed to receive the support they expected from Britain and France, turned to Germany and her allies.

Newly commissioned officers at the time of their graduation, probably in 1914. (author's collection, from M. Youden)

The remarkable resilience of the Ottoman Army in World War I can also be traced back to the Young Turk Revolution. Political and social changes that followed this event had a major impact upon the Ottoman Army, not least upon its recruitment, while new military laws were designed to modernize all aspects of the Ottoman military. Improvements were clearly needed, as the Ottoman Empire faced a daunting array of threats, not only from traditional rivals like Russia but also from old friends like Britain and France. Though the new Ottoman Government tried to cultivate good relations with all its neighbours, to give itself time to modernize and strengthen, the Great Powers had already agreed to divide the Ottoman state into 'spheres of influence'. An Anglo-Russian entente in 1907 led the Ottomans to fear that their traditional ally, Great Britain, would no longer help them against the ever-threatening Russians.

All this strengthened the hands of those who argued in favour of closer links with Imperial Germany, which had been providing military advice and aid since 1883. Five years later Germany had also won a contract to build a new railway to Baghdad (the so-called Berlin to Baghdad Railway) which, though never completed, came to be seen as a strategic threat to British domination in India and the Indian Ocean.

Though the Young Turk Revolution led to a period of political upheaval it also instigated a series of reforms in a desperate attempt to save the Ottoman state from final collapse. Invasions by Italy and then the Balkan states delayed this reform programme, but a new parliament was elected and held its first session only a few months before the outbreak of World War I, its members reflecting the diversity of the Ottoman Empire even after losing almost all its Balkan provinces: 142 were Turks, 69 Arabs and the others Armenians, Greeks or Jews. The great majority were, of course, Muslims but 36 were followers of other faiths, religious toleration having been a hallmark of the Ottoman state since its creation. Even on the eve of World War I it was not religion but recently imported Western concepts of nationalism that were the main cause of friction, and here all groups were tainted – Turks, Armenians, Greeks, and even to some extent Arabs and Kurds.

Nevertheless, these nationalist tensions often had a religious dimension and could result in violence. Yet even today, this tends to be portrayed in a lopsided manner. Christian accounts focused on Christian suffering, and Muslim accounts on Muslim suffering. In the Western world, as the historian G. Dyer put it; 'Muslim massacres of Christians are a heinous and inexcusable outrage; Christian massacres of Muslims are, well, understandable and forgivable.'

CHRONOLOGY

1914

2 August	Ottoman–German alliance signed.
3 August	Britain commandeers two battleships being built for the Ottoman Navy.
10–11 August	German warships *Goeben* and *Breslau* enter Ottoman waters.
September	Russian forces occupy part of neutral Iran along Ottoman frontier.
28–29 October	Ottoman Navy bombards Russian Black Sea ports.
1 November	British sink Ottoman vessel near Izmir, Russian forces cross the Caucasus frontier and attack Ottoman Third Army.
2 November	Russia declares war on the Ottoman Empire, British Navy bombards Aqaba.
3 November	Anglo-French bombardment of the Dardanelles; Britain and France declare war on Ottoman Empire.
11 November	Ottoman Sultan and senior religious leaders declare jihad against Russia and her allies.
22 November	British-Indian forces occupy Basra; Ottoman-led Bedouin auxiliaries seize control of al-Arish in Egypt.

Racial attitudes towards Ottoman troops

There was a disturbing degree of racism and 'Social Darwinism' amongst British and even more so amongst Australian observers of the Ottoman Army during World War I. General Hamilton, the Scottish commander of the Allied Expeditionary Force during the Gallipoli campaign, clearly regarded his enemy as an inferior breed; 'Here are the best the old country can produce; the hope of the progress of the British ideal in the world; and half of them are going to swap lives with Turks whose relative value to the well-being of humanity is to theirs as is a locust to a honey-bee... Let me bring my lads face to face with the Turks in the open field, we must beat them every time because British volunteer soldiers are superior individuals to Anatolians, Syrians or Arabs and are animated with a superior ideal and an equal joy in battle... To attempt to solve the problem by letting a single dirty Turk at the Maxim [machine gun] kill ten – twenty – fifty – of our fellows on the barbed wire – each of whom is worth several dozen Turks, is a sin of the Holy Ghost category.' Quoted by J. Macleod, *Reconsidering Gallipoli* (Manchester, 2004) p. 189.

6 December	Ottomans launch a counter-offensive against the Russians, resulting in defeat and massive Ottoman casualties.
8 December	British–Indian forces take confluence of Tigris and Euphrates rivers in Iraq.
December–January	Allies occupy the nominally Greek and Ottoman Aegean islands of Limnos, Imroz and Bozcaada.

1915

15 January	Ottoman Army leaves Beersheba in Palestine to invade Egypt; Ottoman forces in southern Iraq also try to occupy oil-producing Ahwaz area of south-western neutral Iran and Ottoman–Yemeni auxiliaries raid British Aden frontier.
2–3 February	First Ottoman attempt to cross the Suez Canal is defeated.
19 February	Allied fleets start bombarding the Dardanelles forts.
February–March	Ottoman defence of the Straits is reorganized.
4 March	British Marines briefly land on the Gallipoli Peninsula.
18 March	Defeat of attempt by Allied fleets to break through the Dardanelles; during March the Russian Navy bombards the Turkish coast several times, the Ottoman Sixth Army is established to defend the Bosphorus; Ottoman forces from Yemen seize control of the British Aden Protectorate's frontier.
25 April	British land on the Gallipoli Peninsula and French land at Kumkale; during April, Armenian rebels seize Van; in late April the Ottoman Sultan orders all Armenian soldiers in the Ottoman Army to be disarmed.
May	Inconclusive fighting on the Gallipoli front; renewed Russian offensive on the Caucasus front and eastern Anatolia; Russians evict Ottomans from Lake Urmia in neutral Iran.
June	Inconclusive fighting on the Gallipoli front.
July	Inconclusive fighting on the Gallipoli front; on the Caucasus front Ottomans make minor gains north of Lake Van; Ottoman forces take Lahij, defeat a British relief force and invest Aden.
6 August	New British landing on the Gallipoli Peninsula fails to make breakthrough; during August the Ottomans retake Van from the Russians and Armenians.
September	British advance up the Tigris and to a lesser extent the Euphrates in Iraq, taking Kut al-Amara.

November	Continued British advance in Iraq.
22–25 November	Ottomans defeat British at the battle of Ctesiphon, south of Baghdad.
7 December	Ottomans besiege retreating British in Kut al-Amara.
19–20 December	Allies begin evacuation of Gallipoli Peninsula.

1916

8–9 January	Final Allied evacuation of the Gallipoli Peninsula.
14 January	Renewed Russian offensive on the Caucasus front; unsuccessful British attempt to break siege of Kut al-Amara from January to April.
15 February	Russians take Erzurum on the Caucasus front.
April	Russian naval landing on Black Sea coast results in their taking Trabzon; Ottoman Third Army retires west of Erzincan; Ottoman Second Army starts moving towards the Caucasus front (not completed until August).
29 April	British surrender in Kut al-Amara.
6 May	Ottomans retake Uzun island in the Gulf of Izmir.
May–June	Ottoman counter-attacks retake territory near Trabzon; Ottoman units in Iraq are reformed into the Sixth Army, which also takes Kermanshah area of western Iran.
27 June	The sharif of Mecca proclaims his independence (start of the Arab Revolt).
July	Renewed Russian offensive takes Bayburt and Erzincan; an Ottoman force invades Egyptian Sinai; Ottoman XV Army Corps sent to support the Austro-Hungarians and Germans in Galicia on Russian front.
4 August	Ottoman advance across Sinai Peninsula halted at Romani and retires; during August, Ottomans temporarily retake territory west of Lake Van; Second Army established around Diyarbakir but is too late to assist Third Army before winter.
27 August	Romania enters war on Allied side, Ottomans send three more divisions to Galicia plus two to support Bulgarians against Romanians.
18 September	Ottoman troops attack Greek 'pirates' holding Alibey island near Ayvalik.

3 November	Ottoman troops attack 'pirates' holding Kekova island off Mediterranean coast; Ottomans send a division to support the Bulgarians facing the British across the Struma River.

1917

6 January	Ottoman artillery sinks British seaplane carrier at Kastelorizo; during January, Ottoman forces in Palestine establish a defensive line between Gaza and Beersheba; renewed British advance in Iraq.
25 February	British retake Kut al-Amara in Iraq.
10–11 March	British occupy Baghdad.
16–27 March	Ottomans defeat British offensive at first battle of Gaza in Palestine; during March the Russian Revolution ends Russian offensive operations on the Caucasus front.
17–19 April	Ottomans defeat British offensive at second battle of Gaza; late in April Ottomans start to advance on the Caucasus front where the Russian withdrawal continues, rendering a planned Ottoman spring offensive unnecessary.
August	Some Ottoman forces are withdrawn from European and Balkan fronts in preparation for planned Yildirim campaign to drive British from Iraq.
6 September	Huge explosion in Istanbul destroys much of the stores and munitions intended for the Yildirim campaign; later in September the original Yildirim plan is abandoned and most of the Yildirim Army is sent to Palestine.
17 October	Kaiser Wilhelm II of Germany visits the battlefield of the Gallipoli Peninsula.
29 October	Yildirim Army HQ established in Jerusalem.
31 October	New British offensive in Palestine leads to Ottoman defeat at third battle of Gaza.
16 November	British seize Jaffa.
25 November	Ottoman counter-offensive halts British advance along Palestinian coast.
7 December	Russians request an Armistice with Ottomans.
8 December	Jerusalem surrenders to the British.
18 December	Truce agreed between Ottoman Army and newly formed Transcaucasian Republic on the Caucasus front.

The Ottoman Empire during World War I

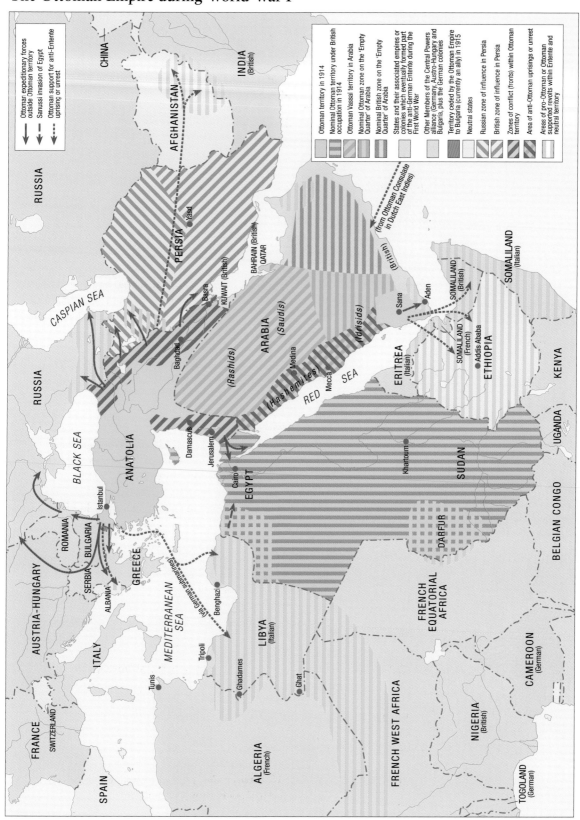

Legend:

Ottoman expeditionary forces outside Ottoman territory
Sanussi invasion of Egypt
Ottoman support for anti-Entente uprising or unrest

Ottoman territory in 1914
Nominal Ottoman territory under British occupation in 1914
Ottoman Vassal territory in Arabia
Nominal Ottoman zone on the 'Empty Quarter' of Arabia
Nominal British zone on the 'Empty Quarter' of Arabia
States and their associated empires or colonies which eventually formed part of the anti-German Entente during the First World War
Other Members of the Central Powers alliance (Germany, Austro-Hungary and Bulgaria, plus the German colonies
Territory ceded by the Ottoman Empire to Bulgaria (currently an ally) in 1915
Neutral states
Russian zone of influence in Persia
British zone of influence in Persia
Zones of conflict (fronts) within Ottoman territory
Area of anti-Ottoman uprisings or unrest
Areas of pro-Ottoman or Ottoman supported revolts within Entente and neutral territory

| 28 December | Ottoman–Russian Armistice signed at Brest-Litovsk. |

1918

January–April	Ottoman forces retake territory in Caucasus, lost in 1878.
19 February	Liman von Sanders placed in overall command of the Palestine front.
21 February	British take Jericho.
9 March	Renewed British offensive in Palestine.
26–31 March	British cross the river Jordan but are forced back after battle of Amman.
26 April	Ottomans retake Kars on the Caucasus front.
30 April	British again cross the river Jordan and take al-Salt.
3 May	Ottomans retake al-Salt; during May and June Transcaucasian Republic fragments into separate Georgian, Armenian and Azerbaijani states.
28 June	Ottoman Sultan Mehmed V dies, succeeded by Mehmed VI.
14 July	Ottomans counter-attack in Palestine and Jordan achieves limited success.
August	British forces reach Baku oil fields in the eastern Caucasus.
14 September	British forces driven out of Baku by Ottoman units supporting new Republic of Azerbaijan; Ottomans retain control of Azerbaijan and part of new Republic of Armenia until end of war.
17 September	Arab Revolt cuts communications between Ottoman forces in Palestine and Damascus.
19 September	Major British offensive shatters Ottoman front in Palestine.
1 October	Damascus falls to Arab Revolt.
2 October	Australians enter Beirut and Damascus.
25 October	Allied forces take Aleppo in northern Syria.
30 October	Armistice signed between Ottoman and Allied representatives, agreeing that Dardanelles be opened to Allied fleets, Allied occupation of strategic locations, surrender of Ottoman forces in areas to be occupied by the Allies, demobilization of most Ottoman forces elsewhere.

3 November	British enter Mosul.
10 November	Ottomans leave Mosul.
17 November	British reoccupy Baku in the Caucasus.

1919

January	Ottoman garrison in Medina surrenders to the Sharifian Arab Army (Arab Revolt).
April	XV Army Corps at Erzurum launches Turkish War of Liberation against foreign occupation.

ENLISTMENT

As part of his efforts at military reform, Sultan Abdul Hamid II (1876–1909) tried extending conscription fairly to all Muslim men within the Ottoman Empire, though retaining traditional exemptions allowed to the inhabitants of Istanbul, Albania, Najd, Hejaz, Tripoli, Benghazi, and the Middle Eastern nomadic tribes who were beyond Ottoman control anyway. Higher education and religious students were similarly exempted. By this time a steady flow of Muslim refugees from territory lost by the Ottoman Empire was another major source of highly motivated recruits.

In 1908, however, the new Young Turk government introduced laws that compelled non-Muslim Ottoman citizens to be conscripted into the army. This contravened the Islamic shariah law upon which the Ottoman Sultanate was supposedly based and, for the first time, non-Muslims had to bear an equal burden in national defence. Only a handful of specific exemptions remained, one being mentioned in the memoirs of a young Armenian, Bedros Sharian, who was called up in 1914. He recalled that; 'In the beginning of the

An army recruiting desk at the time of the Ottoman Empire's entry into World War I. Headgear was a primary form of religious and cultural identification and the presence of a trilby and a turban alongside the *kalpaks* and fezes shows the multicultural character of the Ottoman state. (author's collection)

war the licensed teachers and preachers were exempt from military service.' In fact Sharian was arrested as a draft dodger because he had managed to find employment as a teacher after the mobilization call (Pye, 1938, p. 33).

The normal enlistment age was 20, though men as young as 18 were allowed to join as volunteers if they had parental permission. Enlistment was usually in late summer and in 1914 took place during the brief period of Ottoman neutrality. Once these young men completed their period of service they would return to civilian life, though remaining in the reserve. Those called up during World War I were not released until the conflict was over, while reserves were called to the colours as required. The oldest group was known as the *Müstahfiz*, consisting of men in the final seven years of their military obligation.

Ottoman mobilization was, however, slow and reflected events as they unfolded. These problems were made worse by the fact that the Ottoman Army was currently in the midst of a major restructuring of units while its high command were rebuilding divisional and corps headquarters destroyed during the First Balkan War. Given these difficulties the government's decision to remain neutral for nearly two months must have been a great relief to the army and even then Ottoman mobilization was not complete until early November.

Men were summoned in regional Military Inspectorates, having to sign up wherever they happened to be at the time. In most cases, however, the system resulted in Ottoman Army Groups having a distinct local character; the First Inspectorate mainly recruiting from Turkish-speaking western Anatolia and what remained of Ottoman possessions in Europe; the Second recruiting from other parts of Anatolia, mostly Turks, Kurds, and Armenians; the Third recruiting Arabs, Kurds, Turks, and Armenians; the Fourth recruiting the settled Arab and Kurdish populations of the Tigris valley and Iraq. Other recruitment areas were almost entirely Arab and did not always form Inspectorates.

It soon became clear that the Ottoman Empire could not endure a prolonged war unless resources of both men and material were used with care. Unfortunately, the Ottoman Army did not have a system of substantial reserve units and, unlike their allies, the Ottomans could not rapidly field reserve corps made up of reserve divisions. Instead, when they needed more combat infantry formations, they simply created more regular divisions. There were some exceptions, of course, and the term *müretteb* appears to have been applied to various kinds of scratch or mixed forces not in the permanent Army structure. In fact, many Ottoman troops found themselves forming part of mixed and occasionally exotic formations; one such being a small force of Turkish volunteers and Kurdish irregulars, which seized Tabriz in north-western Iran following a sudden Russian withdrawal in the winter of 1914–15. Their success was then exploited by the 36th, which was itself strengthened by new formations of Frontier Guards and *jandarma*, many of whom had valuable local knowledge.

Military volunteers from an Islamic brotherhood, identified as Qadiri dervishes, outside an official building in Istanbul. (from *Harbi Mecmuasi* 'War Magazine', 1915; Askeri Müzesi, Istanbul)

Recruiting volunteers for the jihad near Tiberius in autumn 1914. The Palestinians had long been amongst the most loyal Arab populations of the Ottoman Empire. (Library of Congress)

Much of the Ottoman Empire's paramilitary *jandarma* were an elite. Formed after the Ottoman Empire's defeat by Russia in 1878, this militia had been trained and structured by the French and although the *jandarma*'s primary function was internal security and border control, every province had a mobile *jandarma* battalion while many large cities had mobile *jandarma* regiments. Around 25,000 men were attached to the particularly heavily armed, well-trained and mobile *Seyyar* which itself included 12,000 frontier guards and 6,000 mule-riding mounted infantry.

Then there was the paramilitary Itfaiye (Istanbul Fire Brigade), which consisted of several battalions, each of around 700 men, armed and trained as infantry soldiers in addition to their duties as firemen. On mobilization the number of battalions seems to have increased, two being sent to the Iraqi front while four were sent to the Dardanelles during the latter part of the Gallipoli campaign.

The Ottoman Government's proclamation of a jihad against Russia and its allies has been widely dismissed as a flop, yet it did encourage volunteers from within the Ottoman state. The Kurds and some Arabs responded, though the effect was short-lived. Another, and perhaps more strongly motivated group of Muslim volunteers were known as the *fedais* ('self-sacrificers'). Initially serving as local irregulars during the Balkan War, most of the *fedais* enlisted during World War I were Balkan refugees, often motivated by a burning desire for vengeance against their Christian oppressors. Several thousand were sent to the Caucasus front and into north-western Iran while a few hundred were reported in Syria late in 1914. However, the latter may be confused with a military unit composed of dervish volunteers who had formed units identified by distinctive headgear.

All such volunteers may have formed part of a long-established but now rudimentary *gönüllü sistemi* which encouraged men to enlist together, resulting in units comparable to the British 'Pals battalions'. In addition to helping the Ottoman effort by working in military factories, women put on uniform during the last desperate year of war, the first female labour battalion being established in February 1918 through the offices of the 'Society for Finding Employment for Women' (Emin, 1930, p. 236). Attached to the First Army, its first officers were men who would be replaced as soon as sufficient female officers were trained.

Cultural and linguistic intermingling

Given the linguistically and culturally varied character of the Ottoman Empire it was inevitable that some military units were very mixed. VI Army Corps, to which the young 'probationary officer' Mehmet Fasih reported on mobilization, was raised in the Military Inspectorate, which covered Cilicia and Syria. In his Gallipoli diary entry of 15 December 1915 Mehmed Fasih, now a 2nd Lt., mentioned that he was fluent in Arabic as well as his own native Turkish. Around three weeks earlier he had described a fellow officer in his unit on the Gallipoli front; 'Abdühalim Efendi is truly a gentle [a play or words as the 'halim' part of Abdühalim's name in fact meant 'gentle' in Arabic] and pleasant comrade. He is the son of a family of Bosnian refugees. On the other hand Mustafa Efendi is a mullah [a person trained in Islamic law] from Konya [in central Anatolia] whose military training has been rather sketchy. He tends to be somewhat arrogant… Call on our doctor, Abdülfettah Efendi [from one of the Arab provinces]… Then go to see Peshtamalciyan Efendi [an Armenian officer] and discuss the general situation.' Mehmed Fasih (tr. H. B. Danishman), *Gallipoli 1915: Bloody Ridge (Lone Pine) Diary of Lt. Mehmed Fasih 5th Imperial Ottoman Army* (Istanbul, 2001) p. 112.

Although Kurdish tribes in eastern Anatolia had a long tradition of resisting central government control they still had virtually no sense of 'national' identity and even their bitter rivalry with the Armenians was a relatively new factor, largely stirred up by the Russians. During World War I large numbers of urban Kurds served in the Ottoman Army while several tribes effectively enlisted en masse as irregulars. Other tribes merely looked for opportunities to win booty, especially from the Armenians who were seen as pro-Russian. On other occasions Kurdish tribes attacked and looted defeated troops, whether they were Russians or Ottomans.

Inhabiting the far north-eastern corner of the Ottoman Empire was another group who are said to have fought particularly ferociously during the war. They were the Laz – Muslims whose language is related to Georgian and who felt themselves to be particularly threatened by any Russian advance. Another people who stemmed from the Caucasus were the Circassians, large numbers of whom had fled to the Ottoman Empire to escape Russian domination during the 19th century. Scattered across much of the Ottoman Empire, they were militarily important in parts of Syria and Jordan, a unit of local Circassian volunteer cavalry in the 48th Division helping defeat a British attempt to seize Amman in March 1918.

Of much greater military importance were the Arab-speaking populations of the Ottoman Empire, though their role in Ottoman ranks has tended to be downgraded or even denigrated since World War I. Even Liman von Sanders was somewhat grudging in his assessment of Ottoman Arab troops, despite his personal experience of their role during the Gallipoli victories. In his report of December 1917 he wrote that; 'A large part of the Arabs may be made into good usable soldiers, if from the very beginning of their service they are treated with strictness and justice.'

Syrian troops were, in fact, soon in the front line, forming the majority of the Ottoman force that launched two remarkably ambitious though ultimately unsuccessful attacks across Egypt's Sinai Peninsula against the strategically vital Suez Canal. Large numbers were then rushed to oppose the Gallipoli landings near Istanbul. Other units were sent east to Iraq and south-eastern Anatolia. Less has been written about Arab units raised elsewhere in the Ottoman state, though at least two of the divisions which defeated a British army holed up in Kut al-Amara in Iraq were largely Arab. In some places local Ottoman commanders had no choice but to increase local recruitment during the war. In Yemen, for example, VII Corps was isolated following the outbreak of the Arab Revolt and seems to have enlisted fighting men from wherever it could.

The position of Armenians within the Ottoman Army was increasingly difficult and complicated, being adherents of three churches that were viewed with greater or lesser suspicion by the authorities. Whereas Catholic and Protestant Armenians were not generally regarded as subversive, Orthodox Armenians certainly were. According to an intelligence report of 1914, a meeting of Ottoman Armenian leaders, Dashnak 'terrorists', and Armenian delegates from the Russian side of the frontier had already taken place in the eastern Anatolian city of Erzurum. According to this report, the meeting approved a Russo-Armenian agreement that declared Armenians would preserve their loyalty to the Ottoman state until there was a declaration of war, but would prepare and arm themselves. Once war was declared, Ottoman Armenian soldiers would remain loyal if the Ottoman Army achieved success, but if the Ottoman Army retreated they would desert and

form guerrilla groups. That intelligence report proved to be remarkably accurate as almost all Armenian troops and officers of the Third Army did go over to the Russians.

Not surprisingly, the Ottoman Army disarmed all the remaining Armenian soldiers and *jandarma* on the Caucasus front and instead formed them into labour or transport units. Following the battle of Köprüköy in January 1916 all Armenians were dismissed from frontline forces in Anatolia. This caused major problems for the Ottoman Third Army because, despite their dubious loyalty, Armenians had been numerous in rear services where they did the bulk of the office work.

Other Christians in the ranks of the Ottoman Army included a few Nestorians from south-eastern Anatolia and northern Iraq. However, after many Nestorians joined the Armenians of Van province in rising against the Ottoman state in April and May 1915, they were regarded with equal suspicion and suffered almost as severe reprisals at the hands of the local Kurds. There were also substantial Greek Orthodox Christian populations along the Black Sea coast which found themselves coming under increasing suspicion and pressure in 1916, though the troops of the Ottoman 5th Army which garrisoned the area were strictly forbidden to take part in anti-Greek activities. The largest Greek Orthodox communities were, however in the western Anatolian coastal regions. Disaster would later strike them, but during World War I these Greek Orthodox Christians were little affected and generally maintained a low profile, except for a handful on the coast who helped pirates and smugglers from the Greek-ruled offshore islands.

The Jewish community had long enjoyed a privileged position within the Ottoman Empire. Most lived in the main cities where there was no tradition of anti-Semitism amongst their neighbours. In fact, the Jews of the Ottoman state generally kept a low profile during World War I, though many of their young men were drafted into labour battalions alongside other non-Muslim subjects of the Sultan. In contrast, most of the new Zionist settlers in Palestine soon threw in their lot with the British.

The Ottoman Empire's increasingly serious shortage of military manpower resulted in a number of generally unsuccessful attempts to recruit from beyond its own frontiers. Recruits were, for example, sought amongst the disaffected Muslim populations of territories occupied by Bulgarian, German, and Austro-Hungarian forces in Macedonia and Albania, though the results were disappointing. Muslim troops, mostly Turkish-speaking, were more readily available in the Caucasus, especially after much of this area fell under Ottoman occupation after the Russian Revolution. Here the 'Army of Islam' formed in 1917–18 consisted of non-Ottoman Muslims, though largely officered by Ottoman volunteers and fighting for the establishment of an independent Islamic state in the Caucasus.

As early as 1916 the Ottoman Army had tried to build up a Georgian Volunteer Legion, which unfortunately became a bone of contention between Germans and Ottomans. Based at Giresun on the Black Sea coast and supposedly attached to the Ottoman Third Army, the battalion-strong Georgian Volunteer Legion was finally disbanded in January 1917 without seeing action. The Ottoman Army was similarly unlucky with its Iranian recruits, a second Ottoman invasion of western Iran in 1916 having included a small force of 'Persian nationalist' volunteers. The Ottomans then increased their number by forming several 'Persian infantry battalions' but these men promptly deserted as soon as the feared Russians reappeared. The same was true of the three battalions of Muslim ex-POWs from French North African units who were attached to the Ottoman XIII Corps in Iran in 1917.

TRAINING

Under the despotic rule of Sultan Abdul Hamid II, particularly promising officers were often the objects of suspicion. Fear of facilitating a military coup also meant that no large-scale manoeuvres were held for many years. The Sultan's fears were justified, for after a brief period of constitutional monarchy following the Young Turk Revolution of 1908 and a failed counter-revolution, Abdul Hamid was forced to abdicate in favour of his easy-going brother, Mehmed V. Nevertheless, the Ottoman Army was still seriously lacking in both training and capable senior officers to carry out the new government's ambitious programme of military modernization under new military laws passed in 1909. Meanwhile, the reserves were reorganized and given more training, with the army's medical and veterinary services being similarly upgraded.

As far as infantry were concerned, the Ottoman Army's tactical principles came ever closer to those of Germany, which had in fact provided advisors for many years. The same was true of staff procedures, the organization of marches, the extent of frontages in attack or defence, and tactical instructions for all units. Indeed, the Ottoman Army's rules and regulations were mostly translated word-for-word from German. Even so, outside observers reported that the impact of this intensive German influence was more obvious in Europe than in Asia – at least until after the catastrophic First Balkan War.

Recent studies of the Ottoman Army during World War I suggest that its main strengths were at the upper and lower extremes of the ranking structure. In other words its highly trained General Staff were competent and aggressive while its rank-and-file were as tough and tenacious as they had been throughout Ottoman history. In contrast, the middle ranks remained the weakest links. Above all, the Ottomans, unlike most European

Ottoman troops training in the Yemen, probably new soldiers raised in Yemen during World War I. Cut off from the rest of the Ottoman Empire from mid-1916, these forces nevertheless besieged the British garrison in Aden. (Örses and Özçelik collection)

armies, lacked a corps of professional, long-service NCOs. In peacetime this hampered the rapid training of recruits while in wartime it meant that, if junior field officers fell, their units rarely contained sufficient NCOs with leadership experience to take over. Thus the high attrition rates amongst frontline junior officers, which characterized World War I, hit the Ottoman Army particularly hard (Erickson, 2001, p. 6).

The urgent need for military manoeuvres was immediately recognized by the new Ottoman Government. Yet the conflicts that were suddenly thrust upon them meant that, by 1914, such manoeuvres had still not been carried out since 1910. Even where company- and battalion-level exercises were conducted, foreign observers noted that these tended to be over-controlled, perhaps even scripted, rather than allowing commanders and units the freedom of action which would have really tested their capabilities.

The experience of the recent war with Italy (1911–12), during which the Ottoman Empire lost the Libyan coast and the Dodecanese Islands, was soon put to good use by the Ottoman Army; its capabilities in coastal defence proving themselves at Gallipoli in 1915. The Dardanelles Straits were, in fact, one of five Fortress Area Commands, the others included Edirne, the Bosphorus, and Erzurum in the east, where fixed defences consisted of concrete and stone forts and entrenchments. The fifth Fortress Area Command of the Çatalca Lines a few kilometres west of the capital, Istanbul, was created during the Balkan Wars but remained largely inactive throughout World War I, its defences consisting largely of earthworks and trenches.

The main communications trench leading to the Gallipoli sector defended by the 16th Division. Deep, zigzagged, and excavated largely through rock, it was needed because of the Allies' huge superiority in artillery on land and from the sea. (Kannengiesser photograph)

Being fully aware of the danger of naval forces breaking though the Dardanelles, the Ottoman Army directed Marshal Liman von Sanders, Commander of the First Army, to protect the whole European coast along the Dardanelles and Sea of Marmara with numerous concealed batteries, while a full army corps stood ready to face any attack. Comparable defences were established along most of the Asiatic shore. Once the threat of a naval landing became apparent, commanders on the Gallipoli peninsula made their preparations. For example, the German officer at Suvla Bay, realizing that he had too few men to prevent a landing, concentrated on delaying the enemy's

Volunteers from the Mevlevi Sufi or Islamic dervish brotherhood, during preliminary training in 1916. (from *Harbi Mecmuasi* 'War Magazine', 1917; Askeri Müzesi, Istanbul)

advance inland while warning his men to on no account become cut off. There were very few machine guns, and almost no barbed wire was available, so he had the beach defended with contact mines and trip wires. A lack of land-mines meant that many of these shore defences used torpedo-heads instead, while the shortage of barbed wire led the troops to strip garden wire from nearby farms, stretching it underwater to trip or confuse an enemy attempting to wade ashore. All this activity was clearly visible to enemy ships offshore, so all trench digging and troop movements had to be done at night. Once the British and French did land in force, the Ottoman defenders continued to take wood and any suitable pieces of iron from abandoned or destroyed local villages.

One German officer, Hans Kannengiesser, recalled the difficulty he and his fellow officers had in getting some Ottoman infantrymen to dig adequate trenches; 'Actually it was a daily battle to force the Turks to do that which was necessary for their own protection... "If the English come we will deal with them all right. Why all this worry and oppression?" These were their thoughts, and often they expressed them quite openly.' (Kannengiesser, 1927, p. 145) In his diary entry for 31 October 1915, 2nd Lt. Mehmed Fasih similarly recalled how he and his men sometimes lacked sufficient protection, writing; 'For days on end, building of Regimental and Battalion HQs has proceeded with adobe [mud] bricks reinforced with lumber and cement. But in trenches, even officers are without proper shelter. Our men, who do the work, are miserable and distressed.'

In contrast, Ottoman infantry in Iraq were sometimes more expert than their British foes when it came to building entrenchments in a singularly difficult environment. In September 1915, for example, their defences at al-Sin involved linking irrigation or drainage canals and existing areas of marsh, excavating trenches across the dry land between, erecting barbed-wire entanglements out of sight in deep depressions, and digging lines of deep pits containing sharpened stakes and contact mines. Here, Ottoman trenches were deeper than those dug by the British, and also had considerable overhead cover. After these defences were finally overrun, one feature that particularly caught British attention were numerous large jars of drinking water placed at regular intervals along the trenches. The Ottoman soldiers' insistence on having abundant good-quality drinking water was noted by friends and foes alike.

Though forced from their trenches at al-Sin, Ottoman infantry enjoyed a fearsome revenge at the battle of Ctesiphon some weeks later. Here they had to defend entirely flat terrain where the water table was very close to the surface. The Ottomans also removed all obstacles to fields of fire, including the earth from their own trenches. At the same time they made excellent use of any raised observation points, however slight. At nearby Dujaila, detailed local knowledge amongst Arab troops enabled the defenders to excavate trenches that were over 2m deep without them flooding – a problem the British invaders struggled with.

Ottoman troops training outside Beersheba in southern Palestine. Behind a line of prone skirmishers the defences consist of separate defensive pits, supported by a line of cavalrymen. (Library of Congress)

Local knowledge was one thing, general levels of education were quite another. These were very varied, not only between officers and other ranks, but within the Ottoman officer corps, between men from urban and rural backgrounds, and from different regions of the sprawling Ottoman state. The American diplomat Einstein found that some Ottoman elite families, though patriotic and willing to fight, considered the way their sons were treated under training quite unacceptable. In his diary entry for 9 June 1915 he noted; 'S. Bey called, indignant over his son's treatment in the cadet school, and expressing his readiness to do anything to get him out of it. The boy is quartered in filthy surroundings, without running water or decent food, and ordered about by hectoring sergeants.' The sophisticated Western European culture of some Ottoman officers is also apparent in Mehmed Fasih's Gallipoli diary, where he mentioned that in his dugout he used to read the mid-18th century French book *Manon Lescault*, 'a novel of which I'm very fond'. Written by Antoine François Prévost, this rather scandalous tale provided the basis for several operas, perhaps the most famous being by Puccini. Men like Mehmed Fasih were clearly a world apart from the bloodthirsty Turks and crazed religious fanatics beloved of Western propaganda.

This did not, however, mean that all Ottoman infantry officers were adequately trained or educated. One man captured early in 1915 informed his British interrogators that 'Officers were trained for six and a half hours per day in barracks'. Some German officers were even more critical, Hans Kannengiesser being unable to hide his own racial prejudice when he wrote his memoirs of the Gallipoli Campaign; 'There were many who had been raised from the troops without having attended any training schools, and there were actually company commanders who could neither read nor write and were therefore not really Effendis... I have also found company commanders who were negroes. Noticeably small was the number of officers who could read a map correctly.' Kannengiesser criticized the Ottoman officer corps for other reasons as well, including what he regarded as a lack of initiative. This he ascribed to the fact that senior field officers were constantly looking over the shoulders of their juniors and rarely allowed them any independence. However, this was not always the case, as Kannengiesser admitted; 'I don't mean to say that all the officers were like this. There were quite a large number who were independent and acted independently, and who were full of initiative and ideas.' (Kannengiesser, 1927, p. 86)

The Germans also had reservations about an Ottoman tradition of training recruits far from their home regions. Many new training schools for infantry riflemen and NCOs had been opened, though their facilities were often limited. There were also huge differences in the standards of training available on different fronts. In general, basic training for ordinary soldiers was based upon extremely severe discipline, initial instruction focusing upon individual skills and then moving on to training as small units.

Because munitions were so limited, each soldier was usually issued with from 20 to 30 rifle rounds per year. Consequently, many

British account of Ottoman infantry training

British knowledge of the Ottoman Army's training programme during the early part of World War I relied to a great extent upon information from prisoners. One such interrogation was described in the British Handbook of the Turkish Army; 'The prisoner, an officer, was for six weeks attached to a depot at Ali Aghlu. Each battalion there was composed of four officers and from 200 to 250 men. The men were trained for about twenty-five days in physical drill and marching and then received rifles... German inspectors visited the depot twice a week. The men were mostly Turks of from twenty-one to forty-five years of age... The maximum as at the Ali Oghlu depot, was 1,200, the number of men being trained afterwards falling to 600. Most men had about twenty-five to thirty days' training before being drafted into line units, those who had received previous military training being first selected.' Anon, *Handbook of the Turkish Army*, Eighth Provision Edition (Cairo, 1916) p. 123.

Ottoman infantry officers with German gas masks, probably on the Russian front in Galicia. (Örses and Özçelik collection)

Ottoman infantry being trained to shoot at enemy aircraft on the Strimon front in Greek Macedonia, 1917. German pilots noted that their Ottoman allies tended to fire on any aircraft, friendly or otherwise. (ex-Süddeutsche Zeitung)

men arrived at the front with minimal skill. Within one division committed to the vital Gallipoli campaign, Hans Kannengiesser recorded that there were 3,701 'so-called trained troops', plus 440 trained and 2,734 untrained recruits. He further complained that there should have been plenty of time to get men properly trained in reserve regiments. These reported their training progress to Divisional HQ every day and, in Kannengiesser's opinion, such messages sometimes contained 'unbelievable nonsense'. For example, one battalion listed as one day's work; 'Sights correction and bayonet fighting', and on another day, 'Head right and turn left'.

Liman von Sanders raised the training standards of the men under his command, especially those who would shortly face the full force of the Anglo-French assault upon the Dardanelles. They and the troops who expected a comparable Russian assault upon the Bosphorus had undertaken almost constant route marches, sham fighting, and alarm exercises. Though the lessons subsequently learned at Gallipoli were incorporated into the Ottoman infantry's training programmes, Sanders himself noted that from August 1916 onwards the need to train large numbers of raw recruits meant that exercises of company formation or larger were no longer possible.

The British assessment of the Ottoman infantry was that they were well-trained and steady but slow in movement, especially in attack, and that they were little used to scouting or reconnaissance. The men were, it was suggested, generally moderate or poor shots though the British did admit that Ottoman snipers had been 'efficient' during the Gallipoli campaign. Other British and French sources suggest that Ottoman marksmanship was generally superior to that of the Allies, especially that of recent British recruits in the so-called 'Kitchener's Army'. Hans Kannengiesser again provides specific detailed information, writing that in the summer of 1915; 'Shooting ranges were also prepared, and we actually found supplies of German ring targets with the head of a Prussian infantryman stuck on. The results were awful! A German range NCO would have had a tummy-ache, but finally the Turks shot quite well. When a bull's eye was reported I used to satisfy myself personally that the report was correct.'

In contrast to the courageous but rather unimaginative Ottoman tactics used during the Gallipoli campaign, the largely Arab troops who faced the British during the early part of the Iraq campaign used guerrilla as well as traditional tactics. The former caused the British major problems for a while, especially by cutting the oil pipeline inside south-western Iran. These operations strengthened British determination to press ahead as fast as possible, to take Baghdad and stop it becoming a guerrilla base. The result was a premature advance during which the Ottomans fought short delaying actions and cut British communications lines. They then defeated the British at the battle of Ctesiphon and followed up with a four-month siege of Kut al-Amara, which culminated in the surrender of thousands of British troops.

Of course, Ottoman infantry tactics changed during the course of the war, as did those of other belligerents. On the offensive they initially relied upon massed advances, sometimes with troops throwing grenades ahead of them as seen during a successful counter-attack at the battle of Dujaila in Iraq. The same tactics were used during the Gallipoli campaign, with perhaps inevitable high casualties. Late in 1915, however, Bulgaria's entry into the conflict opened up direct communications between the Ottoman Empire and its Central Power allies, leading to deliveries of new weaponry and a consequent adoption of modified infantry tactics. A massive new counter-offensive was planned against the British on the Gallipoli Peninsula, using poisonous gas for the first time. Germans experts arrived and the Ottoman Army trained selected men as *hücum tabur*: German-style storm troops. The necessary equipment was stockpiled but a British withdrawal meant that this ambitious attack was no longer needed on that front. Such changes in Ottoman infantry tactics were reflected in frontline and training photographs which showed a shift from closely-packed groups of men rushing forwards, as at Gallipoli, to widely spaced formations advancing in what appear to have been separate 'leapfrog' jumps. In this respect the Ottomans were doing much the same as other belligerent armies.

An Ottoman military supply caravan of two-humped Bactrian camels in central Anatolia during World War I. The aircraft is an Albatross CIII, probably from the 8th Bölüg (squadron) based at Kayseri in 1917. (De Nogales photograph)

A change in the military relationship between the Ottoman Empire and Germany during the autumn of 1917 also meant that Ottoman officers took over all training, under minimal German supervision. How far this really happened is unclear, but under the new Military Convention, as it was called, large numbers of Ottoman officers were certainly sent for training in Germany. Meanwhile, within the Ottoman state, according a report by Liman von Sanders, the military situation was so desperate by December 1917 that most of the army no longer had time for proper training; 'The diminution of the efficiency of many parts of the army is chiefly due to the mistakes of Turkish headquarters. For about two years now a great part of the troops has not been granted sufficient time for training. They have been torn apart, before the small and large units have been properly cemented together.' (Sanders, 1920, pp. 191–92) In fact, the Ottoman Army's entire effort was now focused upon a losing battle for survival.

DAILY LIFE

All sources, from friend and foe, agree that the life of the ordinary Ottoman soldier was harsher than that of other participants in World War I. Similarly, *Mehmetçik,* or 'Little Mehmet' as he was affectionately known, was one of the toughest soldiers of his day. Almost always badly clothed and badly fed, there were many occasions when units which had been equipped to serve in Palestine or Iraq suddenly found themselves sent to the Caucasus front in winter. Here, and often elsewhere, problems of transport and communications meant that only a third of standard rations could be issued, and these were limited enough in the first place. Resulting deaths from exposure, hunger, and disease were appalling. Even in the Middle East, specifically in Syria, men lived on half rations for months on end while the food itself was a thin gruel of flour and water which even the resilient Ottoman infantryman eventually found it impossible to stomach. Because conditions were no better behind the front, food supplies often got eaten by men along the supply lines.

One desperate report from Syria, written late in 1917, summed up the situation; 'The food situation in the Fourth Army is so dreadful that only 350 grams of flour can be given to men and 2.5 kilograms of forage to animals. If communications are not improved it is doubtful whether we can go on.' (Hussein Hussnu Emir quoted in Emin, 1930, pp. 250–51) Field officers normally lived little better than their men, though there could be occasional treats, as Mehmed Fasih noted in his Gallipoli diary on 21 October 1915; 'Delegation of Syrian literati visit Regimental HQ with a gift of Damascus baklava for the officers. Each of us received a slice.'

Troops normally carried two days' rations in their packs, or if necessary three days', but during the Ottoman assault across the Sinai Peninsula in January 1915 each man carried rations for five days. Food production in the Ottoman Empire had suffered a serious blow in 1914 when mobilization meant that much of the harvest had not been gathered. Famines soon followed and British Army intelligence observed in a note to its *Handbook on the Turkish Army* that; 'In war the soldier has little to eat; his rations are 1$\frac{1}{2}$ lbs per day of bread with vegetables or rice. Meat is seldom given, and pay is seldom forthcoming.'

Foreign officers serving with the Ottoman Army during World War I were often horrified by the soldiers' diet. Kannengiesser, for example, described it as 'eternal bulgar, or bakla, or fasulia (beans)'. This German officer described how small donkeys, laded with pannikins or old petrol cans, brought food to men in the frontline, each container covered with cloth to prevent the food spilling. The food itself, he thought, had the sickening smell of old cart grease, though the men seemed content enough. 'This is no real war,' they joked to each other, 'we get something to eat every day.' When asked if they had any complaints, they would shout out individually or in unison, 'Eji Bey,' or later, 'Eji Pasha!' – meaning 'No complaint, Bey' or 'No complaint, Pasha'. Whether they said this with an eye on their own Ottoman officers or NCOs is not recorded. Hans Kannengiesser then described the men under his command seated with eight men around a tin tray eating their meal as a group; 'Each threw a piece of bread into the soup and calmly and dignified, each without haste, recovered it with his spoon. I have never seen a battle for food, no matter how great the hunger.' (Kannengiesser, 1927, pp. 148–49)

Though the quality of food was poor even on better-supplied fronts, some comments by Western observers reflect a prejudice against what was, in essence, a healthy Turco-Middle Eastern diet. Einstein, who was based in Istanbul throughout much of the Gallipoli campaign, wrote of the largely Arab troops based at Yeniköy just north of the city on 16 July 1915; 'They are so raw that it will take time before they are fit even to man trenches. We passed them in the evening carrying their pilaff in japanned iron wash-basins – our dogs would hardly eat it, but it was their sole dinner.'

Mud-brick huts of the 25th Infantry Regiment near Palamutluk in October 1915, at the height of the Gallipoli campaign. (Kannengiesser photograph)

Ottoman troops helping a German mountain artillery unit through the snow of eastern Anatolia. (Örses and Özçelik collection)

Each division had its own divisional cookhouses and built ovens to bake huge quantities of pita-style bread. At the Dardanelles and Galicia these were partly replaced by mobile field kitchens like those used by most other armies. Meanwhile, troops stationed in quiet areas, away from the main fronts, sometimes seem to have been forgotten about altogether. Manisa, for example, was a thriving town at the heart of a fertile agricultural region in western Anatolia and was on a railway line. Nevertheless, toward the end of the war its garrison was virtually starving (Toynbee, 1923, p. 142).

The one thing that Ottoman soldiers would not do without was plenty of good, clean drinking water. Fortunately for the defenders of the Gallipoli Peninsula, their positions were better than those of the invaders in this respect. Almost invariably on higher ground, they also controlled the springs that dotted this relatively fertile part of Turkey even in the height of summer. This was apparently more important for the Ottomans than for most other troops because, as Kannengiesser recalled; 'The Turk is not only a large water drinker, but he knows water and differentiates between different sorts as we do by wine.' Summarizing the particular importance of water quality as well as quantity for the Ottoman defenders, he maintained that the 'Turk' was quite impossible as a soldier without it; 'If we also had been forced to bring our water in tank ships to Gallipoli, and then had to bring it up on donkeys' backs to the trenches, the bodily resistance of the Turk would have certainly completely broken down.' (Kannengiesser, 1927, p. 172)

Apart from clean water and adequate ammunition for his rifle, another vital necessity for Ottoman troops was tobacco; 'I sometimes received from the Marshal [Liman von Sanders] whole parcels of cigarettes which I distributed in the front line only. It gave me particular pleasure, when in the trenches, to say to each man I found actively employed at his loop-hole, "Hold your left hand out behind you." I always put two cigarettes in his hand and I seldom received even a very soft *"Teshekkür ederim"* [I thank you], but I felt how grateful they were, these brave *askers* [soldiers].' (Kannengiesser, 1927, pp. 152–53)

A heliograph crew whose uniforms suggest that, with the exception of the officer second from right, they are from an infantry regiment. (Askeri Müzesi, Istanbul)

The Ottoman soldier's expectations of accommodation were even more limited, the great majority coming from poor rural backgrounds and were accustomed to sleeping on the floor; 'The most they know are carpets and mattresses which are pulled out of a cupboard for the night and lain anywhere on the floor.' (Kannengiesser, 1927, pp. 148–49)

Mehmed Fasih's frequent mentioning of enemy aircraft largely contradicts what Western military historians have claimed about the impact of Allied aerial supremacy upon Ottoman base-camps on the Gallipoli front. The destruction of a flour store by aerial bombing is thought to have caused a temporary reduction of rations in the front line, while French aircraft focused on store dumps at Kumkale on the Asiatic side of the Dardanelles. According to testimony given to a post-war American enquiry headed by General. Billy Mitchell, concerning the effectiveness of such aerial bombing, a Turkish major stated that because of allied air supremacy all supplies and troops on the Gallipoli front eventually had to be moved by night. Attempts by day were attacked by both aircraft and naval gunfire, resulting in dispersed convoys, wrecked carts, dead baggage animals, and long delays. Furthermore, French aircraft frequently attacked the Soganli Dere rest camp where the white Turkish tents had to be camouflaged. Eventually, the troops in this camp – as elsewhere – were accommodated in dugouts excavated from the hillside, though this was probably more to provide them with winter shelter than to protect them from aerial bombing.

Hardy as Ottoman soldiery were, they were as vulnerable to disease as their allies and enemies – especially when weakened by an inadequate diet. The Ottoman Army's medical services were organized centrally and proved unable to deal with rapidly mounting problems. The number of qualified medical personnel was very small, considering the eventual size of the army, and Ottoman records show that the overwhelming majority of the 1,202 doctors were Muslims, plus nine Greeks, 17 Armenians, and three Jews. The 1,353 reserve surgeons were more varied, with 528 Muslims, 331 Greeks, 229 Armenians, 116 Jews, and 79 Catholic Maronites. More than one in eight would die as a result of disease or combat (Emin 1930, p. 252).

One reason why detailed information is still emerging about the Ottoman Army during World War I is the Ottoman tradition of overwhelming bureaucracy, this passion for paperwork infuriating many German advisors. Friction between the Ottoman Empire and its allies grew worse as the years passed, and instances of Ottoman troops dancing in their trenches shouting

An Ottoman infantry unit during its transfer to the Iraqi front. Behind their officer is a bugle band with at least one drummer. (Askeri Müzesi, Istanbul)

'*Allah büjük, Allemano büjük*' (God is Great, Germany is great), as they did when the British battleship *Queen Elizabeth* was sunk within sight of the Gallipoli Peninsula, would become rare.

Even as some Germans themselves recognized, cooperation was made more difficult because most Central Power advisors failed to understand the Ottoman or Muslim way of doing things. Worse still, they showed scant respect for the Empire's Islamic heritage and many German officers made it clear that they regarded themselves as superior to both Turks and Arabs, officers or otherwise. On the other side, younger Ottoman officers with Turkish nationalist feelings resented being treated like second-class soldiers in their own army. Things came to a climax with the creation of the Yildirim Army Corps in 1917. Originally intended to retake Iraq from the invading British, it was envisaged as an almost entirely Turkish force in which Germans would be confined to the senior ranks. Such a structure of command was, however, rejected by the Ottomans and the operation was delayed. Then came a British breakthrough in Palestine, which resulted in the Yildirim Army Corps, now largely officered by Turks, being sent to that front in a doomed attempt to retrieve the situation.

Shelters in a rest area during the Gallipoli campaign. Cut into the rear of hills as a protection against long-range artillery, they were partially faced with sandbags. (Örses and Özçelik collection)

A   **UNLOADING WOUNDED AT THE QUAY AT ÜSKUDAR, 1918**

One of the most famous military hospitals in the world stood on the eastern shore of the Bosphorus facing Istanbul. It was here, in the Ottoman Army's old Selimiye Barracks, that Florence Nightingale had worked during the Crimean War. During World War I huge numbers of wounded and sick soldiers were landed on both shores of the Bosphorus. Many of the medical personnel who tended them were non-Muslims. They included Syrian Arab Christians, Greek Orthodox Christians, and Armenians, though almost all Armenian soldiers and officers had been disarmed following an Armenian uprising in support of the invading Russians. While Muslim nurses wore an all-enveloping head covering, non-Muslim nurses showed some of their hair. World War I also saw remarkable changes within the Ottoman state, including a continuation of the 'westernizing' and 'liberalizing' trends that started in the late 19th century and would be imposed by force after World War I. These were reflected in the clothing worn by some women of the educated elite. At the same time, however, traditional loyalties remained deeply rooted, especially amongst those close to the Court. To illustrate this point, the crudely manufactured uniforms worn by field officers late in the war, such as can be seen on the wounded *binbashi* (major) in this picture, contrast with the splendid walking-out uniform of a *yüzbashi* (captain) in the Sultan's Infantry Guard.

APPEARANCE AND WEAPONRY

Enthusiastic as some members of the Young Turk Ottoman Government might have been for the Ottoman Empire to enter the war as Germany's ally, even Enver Pasha recognized the Army's weaknesses, especially in terms of supplies. On 6 August 1914 he told his new allies that the Ottoman Army needed 200,000 rifles, 500,000 artillery shells, plus various other equipment. This request was endorsed by Liman von Sanders and was soon followed by requests for mines, howitzers, lorries, electrical equipment, uniforms, boots, blankets, and tinned food.

Very little arrived before the Ottomans entered the war, and even during the conflict supplies remained sometimes acutely low. Nor could the Ottoman Empire itself remedy this situation, its own industrial foundations being so weak. Where sophisticated military items were concerned it remained entirely dependent upon its Central Power allies, topped up by whatever could be captured from the enemy. As one historian put it; 'They might be magnificent fighting men, but even heroes need bullets, guns and boots.' (McCarthy, 2001, p. 103)

Liman von Sanders saw these problems first hand, and later quoted from a report by a divisional commander on the Caucasus front in November 1916; 'Great losses are caused by lack of subsistence and lack of warm clothing. Many Turkish soldiers are dressed in thin summer garments, have no overcoats and no boots. The feet are mostly wrapped in rags from which the toes protrude... No wonder that under such condition whole detachments were found in caves dead from hunger and cold after blizzards or other heavy weather.' (Sanders, 1920, p. 131)

Elsewhere, Sanders noted how the Ottoman Army corps sent to the Galician front were equipped to a very different standard as part of the Ottoman government's desire to impress its allies. Even this XV Corps' inevitable weakness in machine guns was remedied when the Germans handed over captured Russian weapons, followed by more as the Galician campaign progressed.

A youthful *mülazimi sani* (2nd lieutenant) and two *bashçavush muavini* (assistant sergeant-majors) on the Syrian front. The wearing of keffiyeh – Arab headcloths – was not restricted to Arab troops though these men were probably from Syria or Cilicia. (Örses and Özçelik collection)

The Ottoman Army was one of the least coherently uniformed forces to take part in World War I, despite the fact that it had only recently adopted khaki to replace its traditional dark blue uniform. A comprehensive tailor's guide had even been produced, accompanied by a wall chart that illustrated what this new khaki uniform was supposed to look like. At the start of the war most frontline Ottoman soldiers were dressed according to these regulations, but as the conflict dragged on, increasingly broad variations appeared in colour, cut, position and number of pockets, and so on. Behind the front, varied uniforms had made their appearance even as the Ottomans mobilized in 1914, including the old *Redif* uniform of dark brown with red piping, old blue cotton summer uniforms, and lighter shades of cheap khaki. In some cases men were still wearing simple cotton peasant dress for weeks after being called to the

Fekri Pasha inspecting a defensive position outside Medina during the prolonged siege of the Holy City following the Arab Revolt. (Martyrs' Memorial Museum, Amman)

colours, only a *bashlik* military hat or a military greatcoat identifying them as soldiers.

What Kannengiesser described as the 'brown-grey shade' of the official Ottoman field uniform was in his opinion well suited to the 'mud colour of Gallipoli'. Not all the men on that front were so suitably dressed, with Einstein commenting on 5 May 1915 that; 'The men were not very young, and their uniforms were of ancient pattern and somewhat shabby.' Things were worse two months later, even amongst those who remained to guard Istanbul itself; 'The constabulary one used to see in the streets have nearly all gone to the front, and are replaced by a home guard of aged men in corduroy uniforms.' The approach of winter meant that a weird assortment of supposedly warm clothing was sent to men fighting on Gallipoli, donated by the good people of the capital. Unfortunately it included fashionable but impractical underwear and shoes. Other sources noted that Ottoman soldiers plundered virtually anything they could lay their hands on once the Allied invaders abandoned the Gallipoli Peninsula, resulting in some strangely mixed uniforms.

An Ottoman infantryman with full kit and Mauser rifle, as he was supposed to look. In reality only part of the Ottoman Army was this well and consistently equipped, especially towards the end of the war. (Askeri Müzesi, Istanbul)

Photographic and written evidence suggests that the situation was not so bad where military packs and other such equipment were concerned. This was supposed to consist of a green waterproof canvas knapsack, a brown waist-belt, two ammunition pouches or a bandolier, a water-bottle, haversack, part of a tent shared with other men, and a greatcoat. One man in every 12 carried a pick, one in three a shovel, and one in every ten a copper cooking dish. The knapsack itself contained a man's complete kit, supposedly including a spare pair of boots which all too few actually had, the weight of the pack on the man's shoulders being balanced by cartridge pouches in front. Under the flap of the knapsack was a pocket for 30 additional rounds of ammunition, which in the opinion of British observers, could only be reached with help from another man. An aluminium water bottle with a felt cover was attached by a spring hook to an eye sewn to the flap of the haversack, but such water bottles were said to have been of poor manufacture.

Leather cartridge pouches were carried on the waistbelt and could be easily slipped on and off. They consisted of three pockets, each containing four clips of five cartridges. Thus a soldier had 120 rounds on his belt, plus the 30 in his knapsack. However, pictorial and written evidence both indicate that many different methods of carrying cartridges were used during World War I, often including old-fashioned bandoliers around the waist and over the shoulders.

The decorated entrance to a headquarters in north-western Iran where the Ottoman Army used traditional Islamic styles of military etiquette in an attempt to win support from the local peoples. (Örses and Özçelik collection)

The tent consisted of brown canvas sheets with eyelets, plus pegs and poles that were in sections so that they could be carried in knapsacks. A tent closed at both ends normally consisted of four such portions, though a larger one could be made by using more. An entrenching tool was carried beneath the bayonet in a leather loop, but this tool was, according to a British assessment, small, light, and almost useless in anything except light soils.

If anything distinguished the Ottoman Army from allies and enemies alike it was headgear. From the mid-19th century until Ataturk's rise to power in the 1920s, a red fez with a dark blue or black tassel was the archetypal headgear of the Ottoman Empire, though paradoxically it had originally been a Greek Christian hat. In the later 19th century a Turkish style *kalpak* hat was adopted by officers and many mounted troops in the Ottoman Army; this being a black or dark-brown lambskin cap with a scarlet fabric top decorated with strips of gold brocade. However, Enver Pasha himself, the Ottoman Minister of War, is understood to have designed the most unusual headgear used during World War I. This was the *kabalak*, often known as an *enveriye*, which looked rather like a solar topee from a distance and was supposed to replace the sheepskin *kabalak* on active service – though it did not always do so. Meanwhile troops of Arab origin normally wore a traditional headcloth known as a keffiyah. The *enveriye* was made of two strips of khaki cloth tied in opposite directions around a frame. They could be partially unwound to secure the hat or to keep the wearer's ears warm.

B

GALICIA, LATE 1916

The Ottoman XV Corps, which was sent to Galicia in what is now western Ukraine to support the German and Austro-Hungarian armies against Russia, was notably better equipped than Ottoman troops on practically every other front. This political decision, intended to maintain Ottoman military prestige and demonstrate the Empire's loyalty to its allies, was nevertheless criticized by many within the Ottoman high command. Our picture is based upon a photograph of an Ottoman sentry on duty outside the Headquarters of the XV Corps in Galicia. Whether Miralay Yakup (Colonel) Şevki Bey, as the senior Ottoman officer, personally checked the appearance of the *er* (private) on sentry duty before the arrival of senior German and Austro-Hungarian officers is unknown. Inset: (**1–9** collar insignia) (**1**) staff; (**2**) infantry; (**3**) fireman; (**4**) *Redif* reserve; (**5**) machine gunner; (**6**) alternative type of collar patch; (**7**) infantry private; (**8**) army clerk; (**9**) private of a reserve force; (**10–13** greatcoat insignia) (**10**) reserve officer; (**11**) position of greatcoat collar insignia; (**12**) alternative position of greatcoat collar insignia; (**13**) infantry private; (**14–18** branch of service collar patches) (**14**) infantry; (**15**) army clerk; (**16**) machine-gun corps; (**17**) bandsman; (**18**) staff; (**19–29** officer epaulettes) (**19**) *müşür*; (**20**) *birinci ferik*; (**21**) *ferik*; (**22**) *mirliva*; (**23**) *miralay*; (**24**) *kaymakam*; (**25**) *binbaşi*; (**26**) *kolağasi* (archaic); (**27**) *yüzbaşi*; (**28**) *mülazimi evvel*; (**29**) *mülazimi sani*; (**30–33** medical officer epaulette shapes) (**30**) general; (**31**) senior officer; (**32**) medical or clerical officer; (**33**) musical junior officer; (**38–48** greatcoat collar officer insignia) (**38**) *mirliva*; (**39**) *ferik*; (**40**) *birinci ferik*; (**41**) *müşür*; (**42**) *binbaşi*; (**43**) *kaymakam*; (**44**) *miralay*; (**45**) *mülazimi sani*; (**46**) *mülazimi evvel*; (**47**) *yüzbaşi*; (**48**) *kolağasi* (archaic); (**49–52** religious officer or 'chaplain') (**49**) *ordu müftüsü*; (**50**) *alay müftüsü*; (**51**) *alay imami*; (**52**) *tabur imami*.

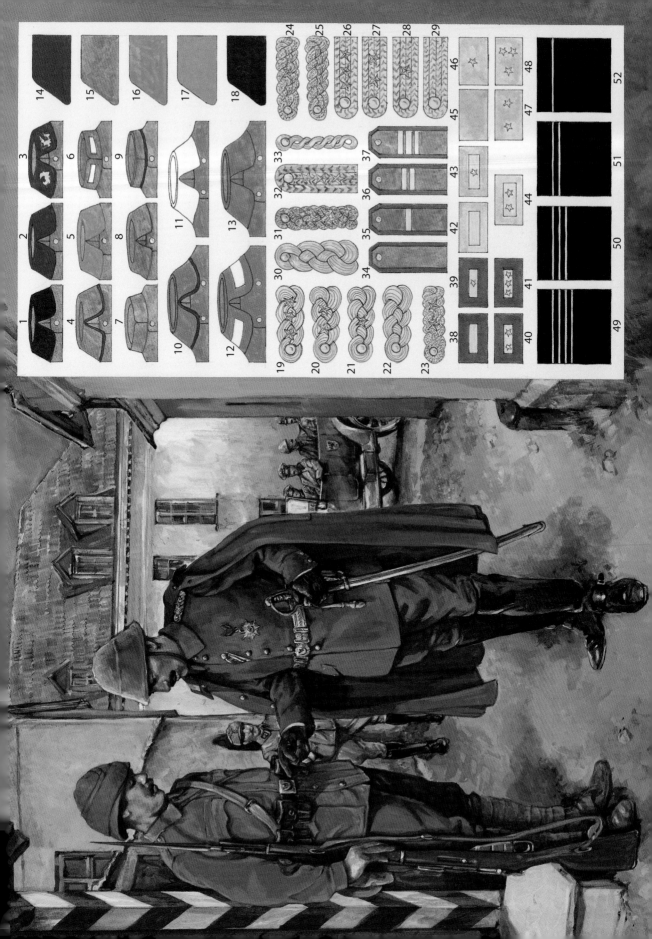

Poor-quality footwear

The problem of the Ottoman Army's inferior footwear was noted by Lt. Col. Fahrettin Altay when he wrote to his father from the Gallipoli front on 2 September 1915; 'The hopes of the British have collapsed. Will they bring up fresh troops, perhaps Italian, and land them at the old beaches – or elsewhere? We are used to it and let them come if they like. In one respect it helps our soldiers, who strip all the British dead of their boots, and now have fine British boots on their own feet.' Quoted by P. Liddle, *Men of Gallipoli: The Dardanelles and Gallipoli Experience August 1914 to January 1916* (London, 1976) pp. 210–211.

Ottoman Army cooks at work in Galicia. The method of providing relatively secure shelters excavated into the rearward-facing slopes of hills was similarly seem in Gallipoli. (Askeri Müzesi, Istanbul)

Of course, the Ottoman Army was not entirely dependent upon its allies, though local production largely focused upon the manufacture of uniforms. Before the war, cotton cloth manufacturing averaged 1,000 tons a year, including what came from new factories. Nevertheless, 50 times more had to be imported. The loss of European territory during the First Balkan War was particularly serious because so much of the state's limited industrial production had been in these regions, so by 1914 Ottoman factories were almost entirely confined to Istanbul, a few parts of western Anatolia, and the Black Sea coast.

Although traditional Ottoman shoe-making crafts had collapsed in the face of European and American imports during the 19th century, there had recently been a significant revival so that, by the outbreak of war in 1914, there was little importation except for the high fashion market (Quataert, 1994, pp. 903–04). On the other hand the quality of local production, especially of military boots, would prove to be a great disappointment. Supposedly of brown leather, the soldier's ankle boots were worn with khaki puttees, though reservists were sometimes seen wearing traditional 'country shoes' with puttees, and by the summer of 1917 even some officers were not supplied with proper boots.

It also became necessary for the Ottoman Army to import uniforms manufactured by their allies, with unpredictable results where the appearance of Ottoman soldiers was concerned. When the Armenian conscript Bedros Sharian tried to surrender to the British in Palestine in 1917, for example, his captors refused to believe that he was an Ottoman soldier, still less a Christian, because his uniform was made in Germany (Pye, 1938, pp. 131–43).

Weaponry was almost entirely German in design and origin, though the Ottoman *Mehmetçik* was usually only issued with the most basic kit, Mauser rifles, German pattern bayonets, and swords. Most officers bought their own side arms, usually European pistols of commercial design, though some obtained Mauser machine pistols. A shortage of weaponry was already apparent in 1915, when Einstein noted that troops were no longer properly armed nor equipped. These problems steadily became more serious, Liman von Sanders complaining in a telegram to the Ottoman Ministry of War on 14 March 1916 that a depot regiment he recently inspected had a strength of 8,000 men but only 1,050 rifles. Furthermore, these were of differing patterns, there were no cartridge boxes, and many soldiers who did have rifles were without side arms or bayonets.

According to British intelligence, at the outbreak of war the Ottoman Army had about 500,000 Mauser rifles of 7.65 mm calibre, plus some 200,000 of 9.5mm calibre. In addition it had around 500,000 Martini-Henry and Martini-Peabody rifles, many probably dating from the war of 1877–78. There was also a reserve stock of archaic Remington and Winchester rifles, though with little ammunition. Consequently it was not surprising that many of the troops in Syria and in other interior provinces were armed with extraordinarily varied weapons, including Martinis which had been modified to use the same calibre ammunition as the Mausers, along with Martini-Henrys, Martini-Peabodys, and Remingtons. In some places the men lacked any rifles and had to make do with revolvers (Anon 1916, pp. 10–11).

Officers were normally armed with swords and revolvers. The Venezuelan mercenary, De Nogales, was clearly impressed by the Mauser pistols, especially those used by Armenian insurgents during the siege of Van in eastern Anatolia; 'which discharged at short range are terrible weapons; the effect of them can be compared only with that of machine guns, since instead of shooting one shot at a time they fire four, five, and sometimes six towards the same target.' (De Nogales, 1926, p. 68) Repeating parabellum *lange* pistols (lugers) were issued to some Ottoman front-line infantry, or more particularly their officers, during the last two years of World War I.

An Ottoman soldier and two cadets from one of the Empire's *mektepi harbiye* military schools, apparently assisted by an interpreter, shopping in Damascus. (Assad National Library, Damascus)

The most acute shortage throughout the conflict was that of machine guns. Following huge material losses in the Balkan wars, the Ottoman Army had relatively few German Maxim and French Hotchkiss machine guns in 1914. It received many more German Maxims during the course of World War I, including the 'commercial' Model 1909 and the same MG08 machine guns used by the Germany Army, but it never had enough. There was a similar problem with grenades, most of which were supplied by the Ottomans' allies, though some were manufactured in Istanbul. Not all were used in combat, as 2nd Lt. Mehmed Fasih noted in his diary entry of 3 November 1915; 'Out of two grenade casings, fashion a lamp with a screened flame so it can be used in trenches. This is how a Turkish officer has to function. If he needs something, he has to improvise. The grenades I used were rifle grenades. Removed primers and detonated these safely.'

A junior officer with his *enveriye* hat partially unwound. (Örses and Özçelik collection)

In addition to standard-issue bayonets, many Ottoman infantrymen clearly used whatever close-combat weapons they could obtain or make. During the Gallipoli campaign friends and foes alike noted that Ottomans carried daggers thrust into their boots or belts for use in trench warfare. The feeble construction and small numbers of their entrenching tools also meant that Ottoman infantry were eager to capture these from the enemies. Gas was not used during the Gallipoli campaign, though the Ottoman Army was preparing to do so when the enemy suddenly retreated. British gas masks were then found amongst abandoned equipment; German advisors recalling how Ottoman soldiers acted the fool with these captured masks. The only recorded occasion when Ottoman infantry actually had to use such protections was when they came under gas attack in Galicia.

Apart from uniforms and grenades, a small quantity of other military material was also manufactured in the Ottoman Empire, there being at least three munitions factories in and around Istanbul. These were said to operate day and night, at least in 1915, and employed 4,000 people. A strategic weakness was, however, their need to burn 300 tons of coal per day. This fuel came from mines at Zonguldak and was brought by ship until attacks by the Russian Navy virtually cut this route. From then on coal only got through in small sailing ships or was brought over the mountains by pack animals.

BELIEF AND BELONGING

Like all soldiers, the Ottoman infantryman's most immediate motivation in combat was loyalty to his comrades. Behind this, some historians claim to have identified a variety of occasionally conflicting feelings of nationalism, Turkish nationalism being the strongest. In reality, even though the Young Turk Government had hazy notions of creating a huge Turkish or 'Turanian' state in western and central Asia, such ideas had minimal importance to the majority of the Ottoman officer corps and none whatsoever to the rank-and-file, many of whom were not Turks. When drawn up in parade or celebrating a victory, those of Turkish origin raised the traditional cheer of 'Padishahim Çok Yasha!' (Much Life to my Sovereign) but, as an American scholar recently noted; 'The Ottoman Army did not cry "Glory to the Nation" or "Turks Forever" as it went into battle. It cried "Allahu Akbar" (God is Great), as had the Muslim armies before it.' (McCarthy 2001, p. 76)

Islam was by far the most important motivating force during the first two years of World War I. During 1917 and 1918, however, the Ottoman Government tried to reduce direct Islamic influence. This had some impact on the officer corps but it is unlikely to have filtered down to the rank-and-file. A call to jihad shortly after the start of World War I, while having virtually no impact upon Muslims outside the Ottoman Empire, was more important within the state. Signed by the Sultan in his capacity as Caliph, and by the most senior Ottoman religious figures, it proclaimed that; 'Central Europe has not been able to escape the calamities let loose by the Muscovite Government in the Near and Far East with the object of enslaving humanity and annihilating the benefits of freedom, a divine gift to nations and peoples.'

A pamphlet distributed by the National Society of Defence was less discriminating in its claim that the killing of infidels who ruled Islamic lands had become a sacred duty (Einstein, 1917, diary entry for 11 May). Unfortunately for those who used loyalty to Islam to recruit Arab soldiers, many of the latter expected to fight unbelievers close to home, as Einstein noted on 8 August 1915; 'There has been more trouble with the Arab soldiers quartered on the Bosphorus. They were brought here under the pretence that the Prophet's mantle had been unfurled, which meant war against all Infidels, as opposed to the Jihad, which is only against certain unbelievers. When they found this untrue there was almost a revolt.'

German officers attached to the Ottoman Army were fully aware of the importance of Islam, not only as a motivating force but also by enabling

IRAQ, NOVEMBER 1915

One of the most remarkable victories achieved by the Ottoman Army during World War I was fought between 22 and 25 November 1915, close to the ruins of the pre-Islamic Sassanian imperial capital of Ctesiphon, now Salman Pak, near Baghdad in Iraq. It would be followed by a British retreat and the surrender of a British army at Kut al-Amara in southern Iraq. In this illustration the *kaymakam* (lieutenant-colonel) of an infantry battalion is congratulating the *binbashi* (major) in command of a regimental flag-party; the *bayraktar* (flag-bearer) being accompanied by two *erler* (privates). However, this event is not shown as one of the Ottoman Army's characteristic flags-medals ceremonies where commemorative ribbons would be formally attached to a military banner. Instead, the men are relaxing or helping medical personnel and local irregulars unload wounded men from camel litters, the 'desert ambulances' of World War I. While this unexpected sequence of successes raised Ottoman morale, it also resulted in a substantial number of British and Indian prisoners of war, which the Ottoman Empire was ill equipped to look after.

peasant soldiers to endure the horrors of trench warfare. This was particularly true of the Anatolian Turks who usually followed their officers without question. Deeply religious, they regarded this life as the first step to a better one, as Kannengiesser wrote; 'The *asker* bears the heaviest wound with wonderful stoicism. One hears only a small whimper, "*Aman, aman*" [Mercy, mercy].' (Kannengiesser, 1927, pp. 145–46)

A front-line junior Ottoman officer like Mehmed Fasih was similarly impressed by the army's chaplains, noting on 28 October 1915; 'Towards evening a *hoca* [religious preacher] delivers a sermon to our troops. It is stirring and appropriate. During the gathering, one of our men is slightly wounded on the forehead by a stray bullet.' The following day he wrote; 'We see Hüseyin Mahir Efendi, who preached to us yesterday, and tell him how much we appreciated his words. He is one of the Professors of Theology at Fatih [an area centred upon the Fatih Sultan Mehmet Mosque in Istanbul].'

The importance of religion was such that it led the High Command to make seemingly illogical military decisions. Medina in western Arabia, the second most sacred location in Islam, was strategically worthless after the Arab Revolt took control of Mecca and thus broke communication between Ottoman garrisons in Syria and Yemen. Nevertheless, the Ottomans refused to abandon what had become a vulnerable outpost in the desert. Medina's religious and psychological importance was too great, and so a small Ottoman garrison remained under siege until the end of the war, Fahri Pasha its commander only agreeing to surrender in 1919. He then left his sword on the Prophet Muhammad's grave and became a hero to pious Turkish Muslims.

A less well-known aspect of Ottoman Islam during World War I was the role played by various Sufi groups. Various strands of Sufi mysticism had flourished within the Ottoman Empire but differed considerably in their attitude to warfare. The Qadiri sect, for example, contained disciplined followers of Sunni Islam who tended to be enthusiastic about jihad, though only in its correct defensive form. Units of soldiers identified as Qadiris and wearing small green turbans over white felt caps were photographed in Istanbul at the start of World War I. A little later they appeared in Damascus where they seem to have been closely attached to the provincial governor, Cemal Pasha.

BELOW

Disciplinary punishment in the Ottoman Army was much as it had been for centuries. These troops were accompanying a German mountain artillery unit as it made its way through south-eastern Anatolia. (Örses and Özçelik collection)

BELOW RIGHT

The *bayraktar* or *sancaktar* standard-bearer of an Ottoman regiment in 1915, almost certainly posed during the Gallipoli campaign. The fact that at least one of the men wears a turban rather than an *enveriye* hat suggests that this was one of the mixed Turkish and Arab units which defended the peninsula. (from *Harbi Mecmuasi* 'War Magazine', 1915; Askeri Müzesi, Istanbul)

Yet it would be wrong to think of Ottoman soldiers as religious fanatics. Mehmed Fasih's diary entry for 4 December 1915 makes it clear that young men in the Ottoman Army had much the same hopes and fears as young men in other armies; 'Fantasize and meditate about future. Alaeddin (a colleague) has become engaged to a woman he loves and desires. Will I ever have a sweetheart? Oh my God, the maker of Heaven, Earth and all the creatures who inhabit it! Please allow me to see the day when I shall taste such bliss. Otherwise my life, which has always been so sad, shall remain full of yearnings and grief.'

Blessing the flag of an Ottoman Army unit, probably in what is now western Turkey. The enlarged detail shows that Christian and Jewish as well as Muslim clerics took part in the blessing ceremony. (Örses and Özçelik collection)

Apart from tensions between Muslims and Christians within the Ottoman Empire, there were also tensions between Sunni and Shi'a Muslims. According to one story, which should be treated with care, a battalion of the Istanbul Fire Brigade, hurriedly sent to the Iraqi front in 1914, was amongst those who were tricked into surrendering to a smaller British force following the loss of Basra. Being largely Sunni, they and their comrades were said to be afraid of the local Arab population, who were Shi'a.

Muslim–Christian tensions were, of course, more serious and ultimately more deadly. Armenians suffered more than any other group, but they were clearly not alone. During the first months of the war, bands of Armenian deserters operated behind Ottoman lines and there were several instances when sick or wounded Ottoman troops were killed on their way home from the front (Sonyel, 2000, p. 101). Massacre and counter-massacre reached such a peak during the war that the Turks were subsequently accused of genocide against the Armenians. However, atrocities were certainly not confined to one side and during the Ottoman counter-offensive in April 1918, the troops came across many destroyed villages where the dismembered corpses of their Muslim inhabitants still lay in the debris.

One of the strangest aspects of the growing wartime ideology of 'Turkism' was its increasingly anti-Arab tone. In the Arab provinces, meanwhile, dissatisfaction with Ottoman rule was becoming more widespread, especially in Syria where governor Cemal Pasha's attempt to Turcify much of the country caused considerable resentment. Yet this did not lead to significant unrest or disloyalty amongst the Empire's Arab troops. Their role during World War I was obscured by Allied propaganda at the time, and by various strands of nationalist propaganda ever since. Syrian soldiers played the leading role in the Sinai and Suez campaigns, and throughout the greater part of the defence of Palestine.

Ottoman tenacity in battle

The steadfastness of Ottoman infantrymen was of course appreciated by their commanders. A letter from Kiazim Karabekir, the commander of troops defending the Iraqi village of Muhammad Abdul Hassan in January 1917, was found on the body of a soldier who was killed when this place eventually fell to the British. It stated that; 'The steadfastness of the troops… in spite of bloody losses, is above all praise. The Corps Commander kisses the eyes of all ranks and thanks them.' Quoted by A. J. Barker, *The Neglected War, Mesopotamia 1914–1918* (London, 1967) p. 333.

Similarly, the high morale of Arab troops during the Gallipoli campaign has almost been written out of the story by military historians, both Turkish and British. Yet Syrian infantry officers featured prominently in Mehmed Fasih's Gallipoli diary, though even he also noted how the morale of the largely Arab 47th Regiment was sapped by huge casualties and too much time spent in the line. Mustafa Kemal's exhortation to his Turkish troops before leading them into attack on 25 April 1915 is, of course, famous; 'I do not expect you to attack, I order you to die. In the time which passes until we die, other troops and commanders can come forward and take our places.' After the war Mustafa Kemal himself said of the Ottoman victory over the invaders on the Gallipoli Peninsula; 'The greatest monument is Mehmetçik himself', the name *Mehmetçik* or 'Little Mehmet' being the affectionate Turkish equivalent to the British 'Tommy Atkins' or the American 'Doughboy'.

It is also worth noting that the Arabs still regard the Turks as better soldiers than the British, knowing the former as *Abu Shuja'a* (the 'Father of Courage'), and the latter as *Abu Alf Midfah* ('the Father of a Thousand Guns'). The proud spirit of Turkish forces even at the very end of the war was summed up in a reply that Mustafa Kemal's chief staff officer made to the British demand that Aleppo be surrendered on 23 October 1918; 'The Commander of the Turkish Garrison of Aleppo does not find it necessary to reply to your note.' The city fell three days later.

LIFE ON CAMPAIGN

An Ottoman infantryman's experience of life on campaign necessarily reflected the unit to which he was attached and the front to which he was sent. Once the army had been mobilized, however, the fact that he had been part of the Nizam Active Army, the Ihtiyat Active Reserve or Müstahfiz Territorial Reserve made little difference, except that it reflected his age and thus the likelihood of him seeing frontline combat, though by the end of the war young and old alike were being thrown into battle.

At the start of the war the Ottoman Army consisted of 36 divisions, to which nine more could be added on mobilization, but the slow and cumbersome Ottoman system of mobilization led to a considerable movement of troops. Thus the men of the VI Corps based near Aleppo in northern Syria were soon moved to Istanbul to join the First Army. The Second Army, which had previously been a largely nominal formation, was similarly assembled on the

ARABIA, 1916

The Arab Revolt erupted on 27 June 1916 when the sharif (senior religious authority) of Mecca proclaimed his independence. Arab irregular forces then attacked the vulnerable railway line between Syria and Arabia, eventually severing it altogether. Nevertheless, the Ottoman Government was determined to defend its remaining possessions in the Arabian Peninsula, it being seen as politically and psychologically impossible to abandon Islam's second holiest city of Medina, so a small garrison held out even after the war had officially ended. The majority of Ottoman troops involved on various secondary fronts in Arabia were themselves Arabs rather than Turks. Photographic evidence also shows that religiously motivated volunteers, such as those mustered in Istanbul at the start of the conflict, served in Syria, perhaps in defence of the Damascus to Hejaz railway. A raid by Lawrence of Arabia's 'Arab Army' is illustrated here, with a *yüzbashi* (captain) giving orders to a *zabit vekili* (junior 'officer on probation') and a *bashçavush* (sergeant-major) of the *fedai* (Muslim volunteer, literally 'self-sacrificer'). Nearby a *tabur imam* (battalion chaplain) is supporting a wounded *alay müftü* (regimental chaplain).

Asiatic side of the Bosphorus while the Third Army hurried to assemble around Erzurum, ready to face an anticipated Russian onslaught. The Fourth Army was not created until after hostilities began, it being assembled in Syria and Palestine with its HQ in Damascus.

Other armies, numbered sixth to ninth, were formed during the course of World War I, though some of them were little more than nominal structures with a staff and very few troops. This multiplicity of armies was criticized by the Germans, who maintained that it required too many staff officers and support facilities that could be better used elsewhere. Movement of troops also resulted in the creation of *mürettep* composite divisions, which did not form part of the permanent Army structure. Even as late as July 1918, Enver Pasha, the Minister of War, created an entirely new Army to be known as the 'Army of Islam'. Built around a few well-equipped Ottoman Turkish units, it was intended to attract recruits from amongst the Muslim peoples of the Caucasus region. Meanwhile, Enver's agents tried to establish links with the Pahlevi family in Iran where Reza Shah Pahlavi, the father of the last Shah of Iran (overthrown in 1979) commanded the Persian Cossack Brigade, the country's only really effective military unit.

Reality did not always match theory and this was frequently the case where unit sizes were concerned. An infantry company was, for example, supposed to consist of a captain, a lieutenant, two 2nd lieutenants, a sergeant-major, an assistant sergeant-major, six sergeants, a musketry sergeant, a musketry corporal, four stretcher-bearers with an ambulance, 18 corporals, a corporal storekeeper, three officers' servants, four buglers, a shoemaker, a tailor, a water-carrier, a cook, and 216 men. In fact, some infantry companies had only 20 men. Each infantry division was supposed to consist of three regiments, each of three battalions and one machine-gun company, plus a field artillery regiment of two companies, one squadron of cavalry, a pioneer company, and a sanitary company, with a total strength of around 10,000 to 12,000 men. Einstein noted on 24 May 1915 that even when a well-equipped infantry regiment with a machine-gun section passed though on its way to the Gallipoli front; 'as usual they were under-officered. Never more than two to the company of about 200 men, nor do the officers look keen.'

Official Ottoman records show that, during the course of the war, the Ottoman Empire mobilized 2,873,000 men, including those in the *jandarma* and the Navy. Large as this figure was, Ottoman forces were often spread thinly over a huge area. Their enemies sometimes assumed that the apparent destruction of a regional Army meant that they could press ahead with confidence. The British made this mistake in Iraq and for a year and half before the British eventually took Baghdad, a supposedly shattered Ottoman Army of merely 50,000 men held up an invading force nearly ten times larger than itself.

Later in the war the Fifth Army, which was supposed to defend the Dardanelles and western Anatolia from further enemy assaults, was weak in almost all arms, having only a third of its supposed artillery, virtually no transport, and almost

Wounded Ottoman soldiers in a hospital ward. (Askeri Müzesi, Istanbul)

no machine guns, while some of its troops had no rifles. Fortunately, the Allies did not attempt to repeat the Gallipoli experience and so this Fifth Army mostly saw action against deserters, bandits, and Greek piracy along the coast.

On the Caucasus front the Third Army was reduced to chaotic remnants by early 1916, exhausted, demoralized, and having lost most of its equipment. Mustafa Kemal, fresh from his success at Gallipoli, tried to rebuild what remained but the situation was so serious by the summer of 1917 he wrote a memorandum to Enver Pasha stating bluntly that; 'If the War lasts much longer, the whole structure of Government and dynasty, decrepit in all

An Ottoman infantry regiment, including medical personnel identified by their Red Crescent armbands, assembled at Batum railway station in 1918. (Örses and Özçelik collection)

its parts, may suddenly fall to pieces... Our army is very weak. Most of its formations are now reduced to one-fifth of their prescribed strength.' (Emin, 1930, p. 262) More recently released documents show that most of the units listed in 1918 either existed only on paper organization or consisted of raw recruits, some as young as 16, while most of the remaining officers were too busy training these recruits to do anything else.

Throughout World War I Ottoman soldiers, especially infantrymen, fought at a disadvantage. They were almost invariably outnumbered and, when facing the British or French, were normally at a significant disadvantage in equipment, training, and education. Officers were rarely given leave, and NCOs and ordinary soldiers never. An Army mail service only really operated in the western provinces and for those men sent to Galicia or the Balkans. As a result most Ottoman soldiers went for years without news from home. Support for the families of soldiers was rudimentary and so the men were constantly afraid that their dependents might be left destitute. Matters were often made worse when senior officers visited the front; such tours usually being carried out with pomp, luxury, and extravagance which men serving in appalling frontline conditions must have found galling (Emin, 1930, p. 261).

Officers of the 29th Regiment, photographed before the first Ottoman invasion of Sinai. Although these men wear keffiyeh Arab headcloths, their unit was known as the Izmir Regiment, suggesting that it was largely recruited from what is now western Turkey. (Örses and Özçelik collection)

Shortage of equipment was a common problem, and officers sometimes had to rely on tourist maps taken from guidebooks. In Gallipoli they found that enemy maps were better than their own. A lack of support weapons was characteristic of almost all Ottoman infantry units. While most divisions were weak in artillery, the shortage of machine guns was even more serious. Each infantry regiment was supposed to have four but at battalion and company level there were often none. As with other forms of supply, the further a front was from the capital, the less equipment it received, and towards the end of World War I Ottoman forces on the Arab fronts were deliberately starved of support weaponry, which went to the Caucasus instead.

Specialized forms of infantry did exist in the Ottoman Army but were few in number. Only two companies of mule and camel-mounted infantry, for example, were based in the vastness of Arabia shortly before the outbreak of war. A larger number existed in Syria and Iraq and there had been discussion of raising them to the status of divisional cavalry. Small numbers of cyclist companies or sections also existed in some *jandarma* units, and there were supposed to be four cyclists in each infantry battalion. More dramatic, though again few in number, were ski troops organized, trained, and presumably also equipped under German or Austrian guidance on the Caucasus front and eastern Anatolia. By 1917 and 1918 these featured prominently in the Ottoman press, though how effective they were is unknown.

Given overwhelming British and French domination of the Aegean and eastern Mediterranean Seas, the number of small-scale combined operations carried out by the Ottomans is quite remarkable. Most were in response to raids against the coast of Turkey by irregulars from neutral Greece, which, according to captured documents, were almost certainly directed by Allied intelligence agents. The biggest operation was when a fleet of tugs and small boats retook Uzun (Kösten) island in the Bay of Izmir on 6 May 1916 from British forces that had seized this island earlier in the war.

These sideshows involved a tiny number of troops. The Ottoman Army's largest operations were defensive, though its infantry were also thrown into large-scale offensives on the Caucasus and Sinai fronts. The former mostly involved Turkish troops whereas offensives against the British-controlled Suez Canal in Egypt involved large numbers of Arabic-speaking soldiers. Though their assault failed, they completed a remarkable march across the Sinai desert and the survivors made their way back again in good order. During these marches each Ottoman soldier had a daily ration of 600g of biscuit, 150g of dates, and 9g of tea. The officers had a baggage allowance of only 5kg and no tents were taken on the march, all ranks sleeping under the stars. The men

E CAUCASUS WINTER, 1917–18

During World War I the Ottoman Army campaigned in a great variety of geographical conditions. Partly as a result, and partly in response to the Army's increasingly inadequate level of equipment, the Ottomans raised a small number of specialized and elite units. These included ski troops who served in eastern Turkey and the Caucasus mountains, here represented by a çavush (sergeant) and an er (private) in fully enveloping snow-camouflage cloaks. They were based upon German and Austrian Alpine troops but, for reasons that remain unknown, were nevertheless sometimes armed with old-fashioned Martini rifles. These were converted to accept the same ammunition as the Mauser rifles issued to most frontline Ottoman infantry. In contrast to such ski patrols, most Ottoman troops on the Caucasus front spent much of the war poorly clothed, often unfed and with inadequate support, holding barely defensible positions. This was particularly true during the winters when the Ottoman Empire's rudimentary transport and communications systems could not cope with cold, mud, lashing rain, and often deep snow.

Ottoman ski troops on the Caucasus front in 1917. Small units of such specialists were apparently trained by the Austrians or Germans. (from *Harbi Mecmuasi* 'War Magazine', 1917; Askeri Müzesi, Istanbul)

suffered less from thirst than from cold; consequently the columns rested by day and marched by night. These were minor triumphs, done without the modern facilities the British required when they subsequently crossed Sinai.

The first Ottoman offensive against the Russians was not as well organized. Launched during the depths of winter at the end of 1914 it proved catastrophic, resulting in huge casualties, massive losses of equipment, a precipitous withdrawal, and a blow to morale that took years to restore. Paradoxically, this disaster was accompanied by the Ottoman Army's first expedition into strictly 'foreign' territory – British-occupied Egypt still being nominally Ottoman in Ottoman eyes. While the Third Army undertook its ill-conceived winter offensive in the Caucasus, a much smaller force of Ottoman troops and Kurdish irregulars rapidly overran the Urmia area of neighbouring north-western Iran where the panic-stricken occupying Russians fell back before them. Despite setbacks, Ottoman forces were still operating in Iran at the end of the war.

Unlike their position within Iran, Ottoman forces operating beyond eastern Thrace (which was all that remained of Ottoman territory within Europe) were under the overall command of their allies. The most important was the Ottoman

Officers of the 57th Infantry Regiment gather for tea during the Gallipoli campaign. Though all save two wear *enveriye* hats, there is considerable variation in shape and the way it is wound. (Örses and Özçelik collection)

XV Corps in Galicia. By 1917 this had been reinforced with artillery batteries, intelligence and labour detachments, a balloon detachment, a field bakery company, and a veterinary hospital. The XV Corps' original two infantry divisions similarly received much needed infantry replacements, which enabled them to form *hücum tabur* assault companies based upon German *Stürmkompanien*.

The Ottoman commitment to the Macedonian front was on a smaller level. Here, XX Corps held the left flank of a front that extended from the Aegean to the Adriatic. Furthermore, the overwhelming British naval presence in the Aegean meant that XX Corps had to deploy an infantry battalion along the coast. Haupt Heydemarck, a German pilot who served on this front, dedicated

Ottoman officers in Libya, where a handful of Ottoman volunteers advised the Libyan uprisings that threatened the British in Egypt and kept substantial Italian colonial forces penned into coastal enclaves until the end of the war. (from *Harbi Mecmuasi* 'War Magazine', 1917; Askeri Müzesi, Istanbul)

a chapter of his memoirs to 'Our Friends the Turks' (Heydemarck, 1930, pp. 89–101), recalling that Ottoman infantrymen tended to fire on all aircraft, friend or foe. Ottoman officers explained that their soldiers thought enemy aircrew painted crosses (the German and Bulgarian insignia) on their machines as 'ruse of war'. Ottoman troops guarding the nearby German airfield did, however, provide advance warning if enemy aircraft tried to sneak up quietly from behind the hills.

Once the outbreak of the Arab Revolt in 1916 cut off effective communications with the rest of the Ottoman Empire, VII Corps, based in the Hejaz region of western Arabia and in Yemen, was to all intents and purposes campaigning 'abroad'. It was commanded by Ali Sa'id Pasha, an officer of Circassian origin, who went on the offensive during the spring of 1915, advancing into British imperial territory where his largely Arab troops soon penned the British garrison into a small area around the main port of Aden. In addition, VII Corps supported anti-British and anti-Italian uprisings in Somalia and Eritrea as well as an attempt to install a pro-Ottoman ruler in Ethiopia. On the other side of the Arabian Peninsula, in what is now the independent Gulf emirate of Qatar, a tiny Ottoman garrison held the mud-brick fort of Doha in 1914 until early 1915, then handing it over to the local Sheikh. The following year, Qatar became a British protectorate.

Ottoman military support to the anti-Italian resistance in Libya would not have been seen as an 'external' operation in Istanbul, since Libya had only been taken from the Ottoman Empire in 1911–12. Indeed the Italians still did not manage to control the interior of the country and, during the course of World War I, would be penned into tiny coastal enclaves by various resistance groups, advised by a handful of Ottoman officers who made their way to Libya aboard German submarines.

These were, of course, small and somewhat romantic sideshows compared to the Ottoman Army's major campaigns, where Ottoman soldiers, like their opposite numbers elsewhere, had their share of rain, mud, and filth. Sometimes, however, this could prove useful, as Lt. Col. Fahrettin Altay wrote to his father from the Gallipoli front; 'When the [autumn and winter] rains begin, unpleasant as it will be in our trenches and saps, they will be far worse for the British. For they will be stuck in the marshes and swamps on the low ground, and the rains and the floods pouring down the ravines that descend from our lines will swamp them.' (Liddle, 1976, pp. 210–11)

Cold weather was nevertheless a major problem for Ottoman soldiers, many of whom had inadequate clothing. As a result many sandbags sent to Gallipoli for use in trenches were cut up and used as additional clothing. The most personal information about life on the Gallipoli front comes from 2nd Lt. Mehmed Fasih, whose diary recalled how, in the small hours of 21 October, he cleaned the sooty globe of his lamp, topped its fuel, and smoked his pipe before touring the trenches. Finding some of his men asleep, he reprimanded them but no more than that, instead describing them as 'poor fellows'. He noted that the dugouts were too shallow, and because the enemy could easily toss grenades into the Ottoman defences, his men must not wander around them aimlessly. This danger had been all too obvious four days earlier, as Mehmed Fasih wrote;

A grenade falls directly in front of my dugout. Three privates who had come to see me were standing at the entrance. One is slightly injured. If he had not stood in the way, I could have been hit… For an instant, I did think I was hit. I had a feeling of nausea, and my stomach felt bloated. Leave my shelter and seek refuge in another dugout. Strip. Find no injuries. Am delighted. But that single grenade did injure three or four of my men… After I was wounded, almost forgot what life in the trenches was like… My dugout is small, with a roof of logs. Since it is exposed to grenades, the entrance is protected by wire netting. Have a wooden bed with straw mattress. Covers include my blanket and a kilim [traditional Turkish flat-weave rug]. Other furnishings include my crystal kerosene lamp, my coffee set, and a tin brazier… Thank God, I'm quite comfortable! My orderly is in the adjoining dugout. He is a good and obedient fellow, with a pure heart.

Turkish hand grenades found on the battlefield of Gallipoli. The weapon on the right is a crude imitation of the British mills bomb while that in the centre is a simple hollow iron sphere filled with explosives. (author's photograph, War Museum, Gallipoli)

Ottoman front-line infantry made use of whatever close combat weapons they could obtain, some of those shown here being converted agricultural tools. (author's photograph, War Museum, Kilitbahir)

Major Ottoman Campaigns during World War I

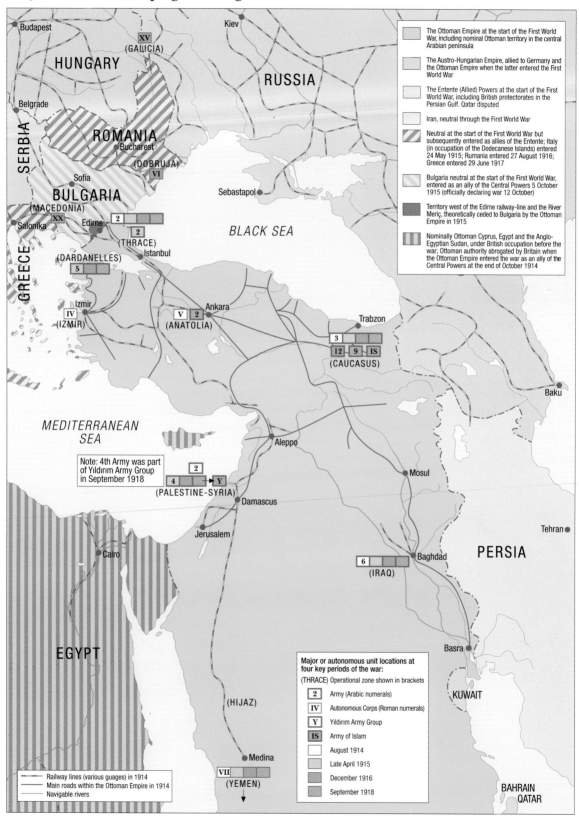

The Ottoman Empire at the start of the First World War, including nominal Ottoman territory in the central Arabian peninsula

The Austro-Hungarian Empire, allied to Germany and the Ottoman Empire when the latter entered the First World War

The Entente (Allied) Powers at the start of the First World War, including British protectorates in the Persian Gulf. Qatar disputed

Iran, neutral through the First World War

Neutral at the start of the First World War but subsequently entered as allies of the Entente; Italy (in occupation of the Dodecanese Islands) entered 24 May 1915; Rumania entered 27 August 1916; Greece entered 29 June 1917

Bulgaria neutral at the start of the First World War, entered as an ally of the Central Powers 5 October 1915 (officially declaring war 12 October)

Territory west of the Edirne railway-line and the River Meriç, theoretically ceded to Bulgaria by the Ottoman Empire in 1915

Nominally Ottoman Cyprus, Egypt and the Anglo-Egyptian Sudan, under British occupation before the war; Ottoman authority abrogated by Britain when the Ottoman Empire entered the war as an ally of the Central Powers at the end of October 1914

Note: 4th Army was part of Yıldırım Army Group in September 1918

Major or autonomous unit locations at four key periods of the war:

(THRACE) Operational zone shown in brackets

2 — Army (Arabic numerals)

IV — Autonomous Corps (Roman numerals)

Y — Yıldırım Army Group

IS — Army of Islam

August 1914

Late April 1915

December 1916

September 1918

Railway lines (various guages) in 1914
Main roads within the Ottoman Empire in 1914
Navigable rivers

47

The degree of suffering endured by the ill-equipped, poorly fed and inadequately clothed Ottoman *Mehmetçik* or common soldier on the Caucasus front was burned into the collective memory of the Turkish people. These tattered individuals were photographed in 1916. (Örses and Özçelik collection)

Life in the more isolated postings was not merely tedious but had the added danger that the Ottoman Army almost seems to have forgotten about certain units. In 1917 for example, some troops guarding the railway from Syria to the Hejaz – famously the target of Arab raids led by Lawrence of Arabia – were not 'listed' and therefore received no pay. Though most received food, others had to live off the land. Such problems reflected the Ottoman Army's archaic communications systems. Being spread across a vast area, local commanders had to rely upon an inadequate telegraph network and, where even this did not exist, upon messengers on horseback. Before the war there was no wireless system, though a very rudimentary network was established by the end of the conflict. Nor were there any telephones outside Istanbul, except a link to the European network, which meant that the Ottoman Army's central HQ could telephone Berlin or Vienna but not its own troops in the field.

The Ottoman postal service was quite well developed but remained extremely slow and soldiers on more distant fronts could rarely send or receive letters from home, the only significant exception being the Gallipoli front which was only 250 km from Istanbul. Instead, older men from the soldiers' villages or hometowns often visited men in the field. Before setting out, they collected messages from families then made their own way to wherever the locally recruited regiment was based. Such journeys could take months and, after exchanging messages with the troops, these elders made their own ways home again.

Medical support was almost as poor. Each division was supposed to have a field medical unit while each corps was supposedly allocated four field hospitals. These were rarely if ever up to strength, a situation made worse by the Ottoman state's chronic shortage of trained medical personal and medical

Ottoman infantry and a machine-gun detachment manning shallow trenches behind barbed wire entanglements in Palestine. The late-style *enveriye* worn by the officer with binoculars suggest that the photograph was taken in the later years of the war. (Askeri Müzesi, Istanbul)

supplies. In fact, the hospitals had a total of 37,000 medical beds, of which 14,000 were in Istanbul (Erickson, 2001, pp. 7–8). There were also significant variations in the medical support enjoyed by different units, the men of XV Corps in Galicia being cared for in the same manner as their German colleagues. Elsewhere, Ottoman troops suffered enormous casualties from diseases of which malaria was the most rife with 461,799 recorded cases, though with only 23,351 deaths. There were about 147,000 cases of dysentery and with a significantly higher death date of around 40,000 fatalities. The figures for intermittent fever were approximately 103,000 cases with some 4,000 deaths, 93,000 cases of typhus with 26,000 deaths, and about 27,000 cases of syphilis but with only 150 recorded deaths (Emin 1930, p. 253).

THE SOLDIER IN BATTLE

Once again, 2nd Lt. Mehmed Fasih illuminates an Ottoman soldier's experience of battle during World War I. He was training his men just west of Istanbul when, on 27 April 1915, his regiment, the 47th, was ordered to the front. They marched by road to relieve an exhausted 27th Regiment and take over part of the line at Kanlisirt (Bloody Ridge) – known to the British as Lone Pine. Fasih's own first experience of action was a bayonet attack only two days after arriving and before the end of May he had been wounded. Evacuated to Istanbul for treatment, then to Hadimköy to convalesce, he was back at the front in October. Now acting commander of the 7th Company, he and his men held a reserve position called 79 Siperleri (79 Trenches), which was within range of enemy grenades.

While more senior officers like the German Hans Kannengiesser witnessed the steadiness of Ottoman troops from a relatively safe distance, Mehmed Fasih did so from the same trench. So, while Kannengiesser tends to be rhetorical, stating that; 'The Englishman is a tough fellow, the Turk also. This the Turk had already shown by lying still under the hellish fire from the ships' (Kannengiesser, 1927, pp. 100–01), Fasih is more immediate, describing a ferocious firefight early in the night of 4–5 November. It started to the left of his position but rapidly spread along the front. The enemy's abundant flares nevertheless helped both sides. Half an hour after the shooting began Fasih heard shouts of 'Allah! Allah!' – the usual rallying cry of Ottoman infantry, which was then followed by an ominous silence. Suddenly the firing erupted again when the 77th Regiment probed the enemy's positions. Half an hour before midnight the shooting died down, so Fasih toured his trenches and was delighted to find that the men and NCOs were doing precisely what was expected of them. He was also astonished to find that his unit had suffered one smashed bayonet and no casualties.

No Ottoman front line diary has come to light from the Galician front. It was here, on 1 July 1916, that Ottoman infantry came under gas attack for the first time. They nevertheless held their line and, in the opinion of German observers, resisted Russian 'steamroller' massed attacks better than Austro-Hungarian troops.

Almost every source of information on the Gallipoli campaign agrees on the Ottoman troops' eagerness to fight, this being especially strong amongst Turkish soldiers. One officer who survived, though wounded, was Major Mahmut Bey whose company was called to arms on the first day of the Allied landings. Officers blew their whistles and reserve companies ran to take up

Mülazimi Sani (Second Lieutenant) Dogan Efendi in his winter uniform, probably photographed late in the war. The material is rougher and the cut simpler than had been seen in 1914. (Örses and Özçelik collection)

Troops thankful for supplies

This letter, ready to be sent home, was found on the body of an unnamed soldier who fell during the Ottoman assault across the Sinai Peninsula; 'By the grace of God we have reached the Canal in perfect health. If I were to say that we have endured no fatigue I should be lying. A march across a vast desert evidently must be difficult. But thanks to our arrangements and preparations the greatest part of our troubles has been overcome. Had we not made sure of our supply of provisions and water the march might have had a sorry ending. Those who say that everything was perfectly prepared did not exaggerate.' P. G. Elgood, *Egypt and the Army* (Oxford, 1924) p. 131.

A detachment of Ottoman troops deployed in the Sinai desert early in World War I. Although the men wear Arab keffiyeh headcloths, the officer in the centre of the picture wears an *enveriye* hat. (Örses and Özçelik collection)

allotted positions. Enemy gunfire was largely focused upon the Ottomans' advanced skirmishing line where the shore was shrouded with thick smoke. Many frontline positions and communications trenches were levelled and as Major Mahmut put it; 'Foxholes, meant to protect lives, became tombs.' While those closest to the enemy opened fire, those behind them knelt in their shallow foxholes; 'With dead and dismembered comrades at their side, without worrying about being outnumbered or the nature of the enemy's fire, our men waited for the moment when they could use their weapons, occasionally raising their heads above breastworks, to check if that time had come.' (Fasih, 2001, pp. 8–9)

As often happens in such circumstances, the heroism of one man came to represent that of many. The individual in question was a *çavush* (sergeant) named Yahya who was part of the 12th Company of the 2nd Battalion of the 26th Infantry Regiment, defending two low hills named Ay Tepe and Gözcübaba Tepe. They dominated what the Allies called V Beach and formed a single fortified strongpoint. Late in the afternoon of that day the Ottoman

 GALLIPOLI, NOVEMBER 1915

On 12 November 1915 Mülazimi Sani (2nd Lt.) Mehmed Fasih of the 47th Regiment was in command of a raiding party at Bloody Ridge, a particularly dangerous part of the Gallipoli front line known to the Allies as Lone Pine. Their task was to destroy a steel plate with a loop-hole which protected enemy snipers. The *onbashi* (corporal) in charge of the actual demolition work was unnamed in Mehmed Fasih's diary, but only four days earlier he had mentioned that Onbashi Mehmed was a 'grenade expert'. While Fasih and his men were briefly occupying the enemy trench they came under attack, two (probably home-made) 'jam-tin' grenades falling between Fasih and the *onbashi*. The latter pulled out both detonators to prevent them from exploding. Fasih's ears had already been stunned by a previous grenade and an unnamed *çavush* (sergeant) in the raiding party was also slightly wounded by another enemy grenade during this operation. Here he is assumed to have been Çavush Mahmut whom Fasih described three days previously as a 'self-sacrificing, dark fellow', who was at his side during the fighting of May. The 47th Regiment was recruited in northern Syria and Cilicia so Çavush Mahmut was probably Arab.

The inset illustrations show some of the grenades and close-combat weapons used by Ottoman soldiers during World War I. Left inset: **(1)** bayonet and scabbard for Mauser Model 1890; **(2)** ethnic daggers used by troops from different parts of the Ottoman Empire; **(3)** Mauser bayonet and scabbard, a later model manufactured in 1917. Right inset; **(4)** converted agricultural and other tools; **(5)** infantry officer's sword, short form; **(6)** German-made stick grenade and grenades manufactured in Istanbul.

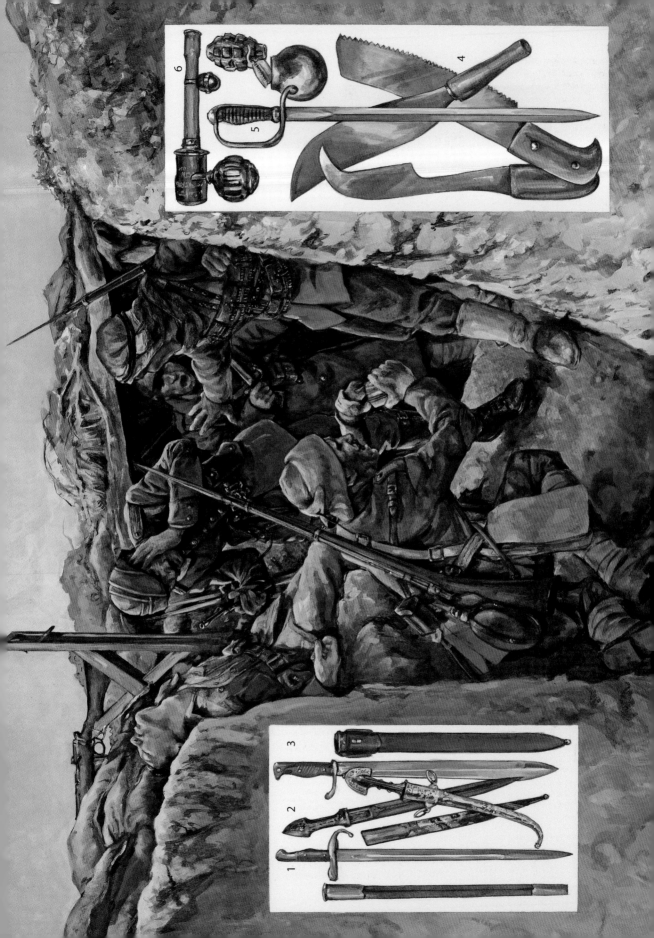

This remarkable picture of Ottoman infantry 'going over the top' during the Gallipoli campaign was almost certainly not staged. (War Museum, Gallipoli)

Remembering a fallen comrade

Mehmed Fasih thought that he had become hardened to the horrors of war, but on 5 November 1915 the death of a young sergeant, Çavush Nuri, showed that he was not. Determined to perform his last duty towards a soldier whom he liked so much, Fasih caught up with the stretcher-bearers and the young sergeant's comrades; 'Obtained permission of Medical Corps to bury him in the officers' plot in the olive grove at Karaburun gully. Pick a spot under a fine olive tree, on the rim of the gully, and have the men dig his grave. We place his body in the grave so his head will be under the branches of the tree, while his feet point towards the opposite slope of the gully… As I gaze at his face, my sorrow overwhelms me so that when I throw into the grave the first handful of earth, I break down… After the last shovel of earth, I conduct our religious rites. As I recite the opening verse of the Koran, with all the compassion, conviction and eloquence I can muster, I again find it most difficult to control myself… Feel like writing an epitaph for Nuri. Here is what I came up with: To all wanderers who may come this way! Should you remember the defence of Bloody Ridge by the 47th Regiment, do not forget Sergeant Nuri, from the 5th Company. He was one of the Regiment's most worthy soldiers. On the morning of 5 November 1915, death beckoned him and, in response to God's call, though he was pure and innocent, he flew away to join his ancestors.' Mehmed Fasih (tr. H. B. Danishman), *Gallipoli 1915: Bloody Ridge (Lone Pine) Diary of Lt. Mehmed Fasih 5th Imperial Ottoman Army* (Istanbul, 2001) pp. 61–62.

positions were attacked by Irish troops, Çavush Yahya and his five squads of infantry on Gözcübaba Tepe facing a substantial enemy column. Yahya's officer fell and so the *çavush* found himself in charge. His men beat back a number of Irish attacks but the enemy seized neighbouring Ay Tepe and attempted to outflank Yahya's defences. Subsequently hailed as 'intelligent and heroic', Çavush Yahya clearly had a flair for tactics and reacted immediately, leading a bayonet attack which at least temporarily restored the situation. The British later brought up heavy machine guns, which enfiladed the Ottoman defences and enabled them to take Gözcübaba Tepe. Nevertheless, the heroic sergeant had delayed the enemy long enough for reinforcements to be brought up, an achievement commemorated by a memorial on the site.

Other distinctive features of Ottoman battlefield tactics recorded by their enemies were the use of what British soldiers regarded as 'weird' bugle calls and, in contrast, their silent pre-dawn attacks during which the officers went ahead then raised their riding whips as a sign for the men to charge – but only shouting their battle-cry of '*Allahu Akbar*' or '*Allah*' once inside the enemy's trenches. The determination of Ottoman infantry was noted by French as well as British witnesses, a captured Foreign Legion soldier recording how they broke through the French wire three times and forced their way into the Legion's trenches where the French fought back with rifle butts while the 'Turks' drew knives from their boots or belts (Kannengiesser, 1927, pp. 132–133).

Death could come any day in the trenches, the horrific reality of this being described by Mehmed Fasih in his diary entry of 27 October 1915. That day a group of agitated soldiers approached to tell him that a soldier named Mahmud Can had been badly wounded. Fasih ran to the position and cut off the injured man's boots, trousers, and socks. After Mahmud Can's foot and arm were bandaged he was sent to the rear. Fasih and his captain then went to inspect the machine-gun position where the soldier had been hit. This was at the end of a path where the gun was fired through a narrow slit. An enemy shell had come through this small opening, causing carnage amongst the machine gun crew. Six were killed, fragments of their bodies intermingled, their faces unrecognizable. The young Ottoman officer then quoted a famous Turkish poem;

Graves, graves, lie open throughout the World,
Lightning has blighted the rose gardens,
Soldiers, soldiers, have become corpses,
Heroes are now carrion for wild beasts.

Comrades of the dead had intended to carry off their friends for burial but this was impossible. Instead, medics collected the pieces.

Stories about 'Turkish barbarity' were common currency during World War I and some were based upon reality in the heat of battle. In Istanbul, Einstein spoke to an Australian prisoner who had been wounded during a bayonet charge. He had survived by feigning death but most of his wounded comrades were killed. The Australian was eventually pulled into a trench by an Ottoman officer who first stripped him of everything useful, and then gave him a pair of boots; 'Three times his few belongings were taken from him, and as often new ones given, for the Turks are extraordinary in this. One moment they will murder wantonly, and the next surprise everyone by their kindness.'

Many of the dead lay for months in no man's land. At first, the British commander, Hamilton, refused the request for a truce to bury the dead but one was eventually arranged. One of those who had to collect the dead was Bedros Sharian, an Armenian Ottoman soldier. As an educated man he was also called upon to interpret, which resulted in Sharian being accused of passing information to the enemy. Acquitted by a court marshal, he nevertheless admitted in his memoirs that he wanted to desert to the British but found no opportunity to do so (Pye, 1938, pp. 76–99).

The patience of wounded Ottoman troops was almost as famous as their courage. Fahrettin Altay was a *kaymakam* (lieutenant-colonel) during the Gallipoli campaign and in a letter written in May 1915 he wrote that, at one time, 4,000 wounded were assembled around his position. Most were sent to the field hospital at Maidos until this came under fire from the enemy fleet. Injured troops normally went to hospitals in Istanbul, including one known as the 'English Hospital', which was visited by Einstein early that same month. He was told that at least 10,000 wounded had arrived within the last ten days and more were arriving. Most were Arabs from V Corps, recruited in the Aleppo region of northern Syria and largely suffering from bullet wounds. Men sent to the 'Russian Hospital' had all reportedly suffered bayonet wounds; 'The men are docile as lambs – like good children, the doctor said – few people when left to themselves are as submissive as the Turk.'

Bombers of a *hücum tabur* 'assault battalion' in Galicia in 1916. Ottoman divisions supporting their Austro-Hungarian and German allies on the Eastern Front were notably well equipped. In addition to canvas bags to carry grenades, these elite troops have been issued with a modified version of the German steel helmet. (Askeri Müzesi, Istanbul)

Nay or flute players of a unit of Mevlevi Sufi volunteers, leading a column of Ottoman troops. This is one of a remarkable sequence of photographs showing various units marching through the irrigated zone around Damascus. (Assad National Library, Damascus)

Four captured Ottoman soldiers being interrogated by British Captain Wyndham Deedes during the Gallipoli campaign. Deedes had served in the Ottoman *jandarma* (gendarmerie) in Libya and Turkey before the war and was fluent in Turkish. (Wyndham Deedes collection)

There were eight permanent hospitals in Istanbul, one each in Damascus, Medina, Sivas, Samsun, and Mosul. Other hospitals treating wounded soldiers were those at Edirne (before it was handed over to the Bulgarians), and at nearby Kirklareli. However, their medical facilities were basic at the start of the war and were eventually stretched to breaking point with major surgical operations being undertaken without anaesthetic. Einstein noted that Turkish women saw work in these hospitals as an opportunity for emancipation, though some also regarded it a chance to meet men, a few even complaining that there were too many ordinary soldiers and not enough officers among the wounded. The Ottoman Red Crescent, of course, took a leading role. It ran many field hospitals, one of which was on the island of Uzun Adasi, which, having been retaken from the British, was used as an isolation area from 1916 onwards (Pye, 1938, pp. 100–104). There were also several convalescent homes for officers and soldiers, Einstein seeing hundreds of such men in the Yildiz area just outside of Istanbul.

The Ottoman Army's shortage of troops nevertheless meant that men were often sent back to the front before fully recovering. According to some accounts the British landings at Suvla Bay early in August 1915 not only caught the Ottomans by surprise but were in an area defended by a division that included a large proportion of men still classed as invalids. In contrast, XV Corps had its sick, weak, or inadequately trained removed before being sent as an elite formation to the Galician front in 1916. Those 'weeded out' were then sent to reinforce the Syrian front.

G

PALESTINE–SYRIA, 1918

In 1917 the Ottoman Army assembled the Yildirim (Lightning) Army Group. It was intended to roll back the British advance in Iraq and then hopefully take advantage of the Russian Revolution to carve out a new Turkish Empire in the heart of Asia. In fact, the collapse of Ottoman resistance around Gaza in southern Palestine meant that the Yildirim Army Group was rushed to Syria where it helped slow the British advance until late 1918. Relatively well equipped as it was, including some of the few Ottoman *hücum tabur* 'assault units' to be issued with a modified version of the German steel helmet, the Yildirim and other Ottoman forces in Palestine and Syria were now hugely outnumbered, outgunned, out-supplied, and had minimal air cover.

The inset illustrations show some of the personal weapons and machine guns used by Ottoman infantry during World War I: **(1)** 7.65mm Mauser M1893, the standard infantry rifle of the Ottoman infantry during the First World War. **(2)** German Maxim Commercial Model 1909, 7.65mm with light 'commercial' tripod, the most widely used machine gun in the Ottoman Army during the First World War.

The fate of Ottoman soldiers who were taken prisoner differed enormously depending upon where they were captured. Those who fell into British or French hands could expect relatively humane treatment, though a Frenchman named Jean Pierre Bory who was aboard a troopship that carried POWs recalled that while the handful of Ottoman officers were accommodated in cabins, several hundred ordinary Ottoman soldiers were thrust into the hold with a large barrel of water from which to drink and dress their wounds (Liddle, 1976, p. 139).

The Red Crescent Society exchanged records of prisoners through the Red Cross Headquarters in Switzerland, while also channelling correspondence and care packages. It was also an intermediary for the inspection of POW camps and any exchange or repatriation of prisoners (Emin, 1930, pp. 255–56). With around 120,000 Ottoman military prisoners in British hands alone, the Ottoman Red Crescent was in no position to offer very much assistance but around 100,000 packages were sent to Ottoman POWs each year.

Ottoman soldiers who fell into Russian hands had little chance of survival. Few returned home, and did so with appalling stories of neglect and massacre. Some reappeared after the Russian Revolution, trudging homewards through the Balkans and Georgia or turning up at various Russian and Ukrainian seaports. In fact, 1,457 officers and 17,715 men were at one time reported alive in Russian camps, some having been caged with German POWs near Moscow. Yet of these known prisoners, only 2,260 ever reached home, along with 6,750 soldiers and 2,250 civilians whose fate had previously been unknown (Erickson, 2001, p. 189).

Ottoman troops captured by the Russians on the Caucasus front, probably as a result of Enver Pasha's disastrous winter offensive late in 1914. Only a small minority survived to return home at the end of World War I. (author's collection and Corbis)

Christian Ottoman soldiers who were taken prisoner received better treatment and as early as 1916 the Allies considered recruiting captured Armenians into their own forces. One of these was Bedros Sharian who, having finally getting himself captured in Palestine in June 1918, was employed by the British as an interpreter. He even met men from his own 16th Division who had been captured in Syria (Pye, 1938, pp. 150–51), but whether they were as glad to see him as his memoirs suggest remain doubtful.

Other organizations also attempted to support POWs, the wounded, and bereaved families but such relief was neither general nor very effective. The luckiest, perhaps, were those disabled soldiers who obtained monopoly rights to sell tobacco in villages or particular quarters of town (Emin, 1930, p. 255). Another dispenser of wartime relief was the Society for National Defence which collected clothes and supplies for soldiers and beds for hospitals, made comforts for the wounded, and helped destitute families (Emin, 1930, pp. 259–60). Then there was the Women's Aid Society for Soldiers' Families, established in 1915, which tried to support 15,179 families of men at the front, distributing 500 tons of food to 41,014 registered dependents. This Women's Aid Society also constructed a replica trench with barbed-wire entanglements and communications saps which the people of Istanbul could visit for a small fee.

Turkish and Arab troops defend a trench on the Gallipoli peninsula. This staged photograph was almost certainly taken very early in the campaign, perhaps even before the Allied landings began. (Süddeutsche Zeitung)

The total losses suffered by the Ottoman Army and population as a whole during World War I remain unclear. Most of the battles in which the Ottoman Army played a major role were relatively short, though intense, and were rarely preceded by sustained artillery bombardment. There was also less use of machine guns, and poisonous gas was hardly ever involved. However, geography and weather could cause intense suffering and high casualties, with disease the greatest killer. All this being said, however, the actual combat-related loss ratio suffered by the Ottoman Army during World War I (10.6 per cent of those involved) was similar to that of other armies (Emin, 1930, p. 215).

Combat losses were only a small part of the suffering, and around a quarter of those mobilized may have died during the war. The ratio of dead to wounded was also a shocking two to one, and of a probable total of 2,873,000 enlisted into the armed forces, 243,598 are known to have died in combat or as a result of wounds sustained. Those missing in action numbered 61,487 and those who died of disease 466,759. Thus the total of dead or missing was 771,844. In addition there were an estimated 500,000 deserters (Erickson, 2001, pp. 208–11) and the Turkish historian Ahmet Emin Yalman has suggested that, without mass desertions in the final years of war, 'the survival of the Turkish nation might have become problematical' (Emin, 1930, p. 253).

Recovering dead and wounded

A truce to bury the dead was arranged on the Gallipoli front though, according to the American diplomat Lewis Einstein, it did not start well. He noted in his diary entry for 5 June 1915; 'I heard this morning details of the armistice to bury the dead at Ari Burnu. After five days of fighting the ground between the lines was covered with bodies. On the Allied side a Red Cross flag was put up, which was followed by a Red Crescent from the Turks. Then an English officer advanced, only to be fired on by a Turkish battery. He retired, and a Turkish officer came out, when in turn an English sniper fired. Neither side could blame the other. During the nine hours' armistice the English showed themselves freely, while the Turks were kept under cover, not to give away their numbers or the position of their trenches. Some of the wounded whom the Turks picked up were still alive, in spite of their five days exposure without food, and with wounds undressed.' L. Einstein, *Inside Constantinople: A Diplomat's Diary during the Dardanelles Expedition April–September 1915* (London, 1917).

MUSEUMS, RE-ENACTMENT AND COLLECTING

The biggest museum containing artefacts from the Ottoman Empire's participation in World War I is, of course, the Askeri Müzesi (Military Museum) in the Harbiye district of Istanbul. This also has a substantial library and photographic collection. Those who are interested in other aspects of Turkey's armed forces during this conflict should visit the Deniz Müzesi (Naval Museum) in the nearby Beşiktaş district and the Hava Kuvvetleri Müzesi (Air Force Museum) at Yesilköy, a few kilometres west of the city.

Memories of Turkish suffering during World War I remain strong. The well-known image of half-starved and half-frozen soldiers on the Caucasus front was recreated in this patriotic poster in 2008, though the figures were incongruously transferred to an Ottoman Army air squadron during the Gallipoli campaign of 1915. (author's photograph)

Five 'battle ribbons' of the kind given to a military unit that had particularly distinguished itself in combat. They would be attached to the unit's banner and are all dated 1332–1333 on the *Hijri* calendar, covering the Gallipoli campaign of 1915. (author's photograph, Castle Museum, Canakkale)

Smaller and more specialized museums can be found in the area of Ottoman Turkey's most significant victory during World War I, the defence of the Dardanelles. A *harp müzesi* (war museum) is located in the fascinating little port-town of Gallipoli itself. Further down the peninsula the early Ottoman castle at Kilitbahir contains another interesting collection of artefacts, either found on battlefields or donated by veterans or their families. A third collection of objects dating from World War I, as well as an interactive display, can be found a short ferry-ride away in the fortress at Canakkale. Other Ottoman military objects from World War I can be found in various other museums, some in Syria, but have not been assembled into specific displays.

Very few Ottoman uniforms from World War I are known to survive, though some may still exist as family heirlooms. The tunic and *enveriye* hat seen here are made of extremely coarse cloth, as was typical for the uniforms of ordinary soldiers and NCOs. (author's photograph, War Museum, Gallipoli)

As far as is known, no re-enactment groups have yet been established to portray the lives and actions of Ottoman soldiers during World War I. The lack of interest is in stark contrast to a widespread interest in collecting objects associated with the Ottoman Empire during this period, not only in Turkey but also in some of its neighbours. Photographs, bayonets, badges, buckles, postcards, and other such objects appear for sale across Turkey and the Middle East, but prices have risen steeply in recent years. In the author's experience, the antique or 'junk' shops of the Old City of Damascus are the best places to look, though even here the prices are getting quite high. Those who know what they are looking for might do better looking in bric-a-brac shops in smaller towns off the beaten track in Turkey, Syria, and other countries neighbouring Turkey.

BIBLIOGRAPHY

(Anon.), *Handbook of the Turkish Army, Eighth Provision Edition* (Cairo, 1916; reprinted London, 1996)

De Nogales, R., *Four Years Beneath the Crescent* (London, 1926)

Einstein, L., *Inside Constantinople: A Diplomat's Diary during the Dardanelles Expedition on April–September 1915* (London, 1917)

Emin, A. (Yalman), *Turkey in the World War* (Newhaven, 1930)

Erickson, E. J., *Gallipoli and the Middle East 1914–1918* (London, 2008)

Erickson, E. J., *Ordered to Die: A History of the Ottoman Army in World War I* (Westport, 2001)

Fasih, M. (tr. H. B. Danishman), *Gallipoli 1915: Bloody Ridge (Lone Pine) Diary of Lt. Mehmed Fasih 5th Imperial Ottoman Army Gallipoli 1915* (Istanbul, 2001)

Heydemarck, H., (tr. C. W. Sykes), *War Flying in Macedonia* (London, 1930)

Kannengeisser, H., *The Campaign in Gallipoli* (London, 1927)

Kazemzadeh, F., *The Struggle for Transcaucasia, 1914–1921* (New York, 1951)

Kressenstein, Kress von, *Mit den Turken zum Suezkanal* (Berlin, 1938)

Larcher, M., *La Guerre Turque dans la Guerre Mondiale* (Paris, 1926)

Liddle, P., *Men of Gallipoli: The Dardanelles and Gallipoli Experience August 1914 to January 1916* (London, 1976)

Macleod, J., *Reconsidering Gallipoli* (Manchester, 2004)

Mc Carthy, J., *The Ottoman Peoples and the End of Empire* (London, 2001)

Murphy, C. C. R., *Soldiers of the Prophet* (London, 1927)

Örses, T., and N. Özçelik, I. *Dünya Savashi'nda Türk Askerî Kiyafetleri* (Istanbul, 2007)

Pye, E., *Prisoner of War 31,163 Bedros M. Sharian* (New York, 1938)

Quataert, D., 'Part IV, The Age of Reforms 1812–1914', in H. Inalcik and D. Quataert (eds.), *An Economic and Social History of the Ottoman Empire 1300–1914* (Cambridge, 1994)

Sanders, O. Liman von, *Five Years in Turkey* (Annapolis, 1920)

Skander Beg, 'The Battles of Salt, Aman and Jordan from Turkish Sources', *Journal of the Royal United Services Institute*, 69 (1924) pp. 334–343 and pp. 488–498

Sonyel, S., *The Great War and the Tragedy of Anatolia* (Ankara, 2000)

Toynbee, A. J., *The Western Question in Greece and Turkey* (London, 1923)

GLOSSARY

Alay	Regiment
Alay emini	Regimental paymaster
Alay kâtibi	Regimental secretary
Asker	Soldier
Aspiranti	Officer candidate of Lebanon militia (archaic term from Italian)
Bashçavush	Sergeant major
Bashçavush muavini	Assistant sergeant major, quartermaster sergeant (recently replacing *bölüg emini*)
Bashlik	Military hat
Bayraktar	Colour- or standard-bearer
Bey	Title of social or political distinction
Binbashi	Major
Bölüg	Company (army)
Bölüg emini	Quartermaster sergeant (recently replaced by *bashçavush muavini*)
Cavush	Sergeant
Cerrah	Surgeon
Effendi	Term of social status, commonly meaning 'literate' man
Enveriye	Colloquial name for *kabalak* military hat made of wound cloth
Erkâniharbiye	Military staff
Esvap emini	Quartermaster
Fedai	Volunteer, patriot, 'self-sacrificer'
Ferik	Lieutenant-general (archaic term)
Firka	Division
Gönüllü	Volunteer
Havan	Mortar

Hoca	Islamic religious teacher
Hücum Tabur	Assault battalion
Ihtiyat	Reserve, reservist
Imam	Muslim chaplain (regimental or battalion)
Itfaiye	Istanbul Fire Brigade
Jandarma	Paramilitary gendarmerie police
Kabalak	Military hat made of wound cloth, commonly called an *enveriye*
Kagni	Two-wheeled ox-cart
Kalpak	Military hat made of lamb skin
Kaymakam	Lieutenant-colonel
Keffiyeh	Arab headcloth
Kol	Column
Kolagasi	Officer rank between *binbashi* and *yüzbashi*, discontinued shortly before the outbreak of World War I but still used for vice-majors of Lebanese militia
Kolordu	Army corps
Kumbarasi	Grenade (archaic term)
Liva	Brigade (military unit) or major-general (officer rank)
Maresciali	Senior NCO of Lebanon militia (archaic term from Italian)
Mehmetçik	'Little Mehmet', nickname given to the World War I Turkish common soldier
Mektepi harbiye	Military school
Miralay	Colonel
Molla	Person trained in Islamic law
Muezzin	Muslim cleric summoning the faithful to prayer
Müftü	Mufti, Muslim chaplain of large unit, regiment or battalion
Mülazimi evvel	Lieutenant